Learning to Move from Messy Moments to Happy Places

Gaye Lindfors

This is Livin'! Learning to Move from Messy Moments to Happy Places

ISBN: 978-1540750549

Library of Congress Control Number: 2017902866
CreateSpace Independent Publishing Platform, North Charleston, SC

Printed in the United States of America
Book design and typesetting by Stephanie Hofhenke, String Marketing, Inc.
Cover design: Stephanie Hofhenke and Tara Curtin, String Marketing, Inc.
And Kelsey Charron, Gaye's Favorite Oldest Niece

In Memory of my Dad

George P. Nornes

You showed me how to find the Happy
Places that create great moments,
which turned into great days,
which turned into a great life.
I miss you and love you.

In Honor of my Mom

Joyce Nornes

You show me how to live Proverbs 3:5-6 …
"Trust in the Lord with all your heart…"
You consistently remind us that God loves
us, and He is always faithful.
I love you.

What an honor to be your daughter.

And for Steve

Doing life with you is the best
part of my world.
This is livin'!

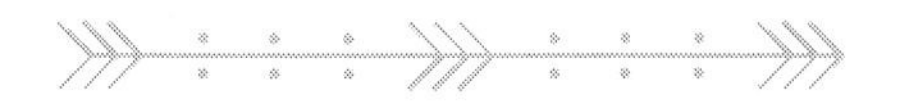

When I am passionate about a topic, or desperate to convey how very deeply I care about people in my life, I can get carried away with exclamation marks and hyper-excited words. So, this page of thank-you's should be filled with those marks and those words. But better writers than I advise to pull it back, tone it down, and write my acknowledgements with a little less fanfare. So, I did. (But go ahead and imagine a page covered with colorful, bold fonts, yellow highlighted phrases, and lots and lots and lots of very effusive words.)

This book wouldn't be possible without the friends noted here. They picked me up and dusted me off in my messiest moments, and brought the fun and joy to my happy places. Thank you.

Mary MacDonell Belisle, you sure know what to do with words. You add clarity to my writing, and this is a better book because of that. Thank you for editing this book while leaving my voice on the pages. Once again, I am grateful to have worked with you.

Mary Miller, Mary Friedmann, and Mary Lou Gorres (AKA Mary, Mary, and Mary with a Lou) – you make a difference! Your friendships remind me of what *"I'm there for you, girlfriend!"* looks like. When I got so tired of my own words *("blah blah blah!")*, you were there to pick me up, pat me on my back-end, and tell me to get back out there and keep writing. Your encouragement means more to me than you'll ever know. Thank you.

Wendie Pett, thank you for your encouragement, your business ideas, and for being my prayer partner. And! Thank you for helping me realize that cooking doesn't have to result in a bad day! You showed me that my kitchen can be a happy place. You're a miracle worker.

Stephanie Hofhenke, you help me figure out what's going on in my heart and in my head. What a gift to call you Friend. Prayer partner. Colleague. I can't imagine doing my speaking and writing – or my livin' – without you in the center of it. Your design and creativity turn simple into stunning, and average into fabulous. Thank you.

Julie and Lori, you are just the best. I mean, really. You are. You are my constant and faithful companions in my messy moments and happy places. Laughing with you is one of the best definitions of "This is livin'!" Always sisters. Always friends.

Steve, you are grace in blue jeans. I'm so lucky to be married to you. Thank you for loving me so unconditionally. You really are something … there's only one "you."

A Note from Jaye

Oh, yes. We've all experienced it.
That day that seems longer than a Minnesota winter and more challenging than putting on your skinny jeans after Thanksgiving dinner. *(As if I'd even own a pair of skinny jeans!)*

It's not just a bad day. It's a "you've-got-to-be-kidding-me!" day. We pray for enough energy to take the next step and long for the day to end. Immediately.

On those days that cause my *"Arrgghh!"* to be even louder and more strident, my whining and complaining and frustration fill up my space and clutter my thinking.

And yet…
There is no place in God's Good Book that says we are intended to live that way. Nowhere does it say we are called to a place of whining or discouragement. I can't find even one verse where Jesus tells us that life is horrible and the best we can do is just plow through it.

The Words tell us something quite the opposite in John 10:10: "I have come that [you] may have life, and have it to the full." One of my favorite translations, The Message, says it this way: "I came so [you] can have real and eternal life, more and better

life than [you] ever dreamed of."
Yup. That's the kind of life I want to live.
A full life.
More and better than I ever dreamed of.

So, how? How do I live like that?
How do I live a full life when really crummy things sometimes happen? When a root canal would feel better than the hurt that stings my heart? When it appears that I need a passport and transcontinental travel arrangements to even *find* my happy place?

I wish I had it all figured out. And I wish there was a magic wand that could be waived over all our future bad days, turning our lives into an eternal happy place with no worries about real life stuff. A happy place where nothing bad ever touches those we love.

Sigh.
That's not going to happen.

But there are a few things I've learned that have helped me move through the daily ups and downs with greater strength, filled with more hope, and fewer melt-downs.

First, I remember: This. Is. A. Moment. A messy moment? Yes. But only a moment.
Whether it's a long or short moment, God knows what's going on and He will either change the situation or change my heart (if I let Him). He will meet me right where I am—right where I need Him to be. The moment can change. And it can get better.

Then, I remember that I have an extraordinary amount of influence on how I respond to the situation. Or don't respond. My friend, Stephanie, reminded me of this over chips and salsa, and helped me figure out how to move more quickly into a healthier, more joy-filled, happy place. It looks like this:

1. The situation happens *(Waaaahhhh!).*
2. Clarify what I'm noticing in my reaction; what is my perspective?
3. Change my perspective; choose to change how I feel about the situation.
4. Change my behaviors around the situation.
5. Move to a new place—a happy place; reset.

In these pages, I've shared some of my "messy to happy place" moments. Those times when I've messed up and discovered that moving to a different place wasn't always difficult, but it always required me to make a choice. It was in those moments and many more moments like them, that my faith has grown while I'm growing up.

When I consider the power of changing perspective to live a full, rich life, my thoughts automatically turn towards my dad. I have never seen anyone live a more joy-filled, full life than he did. There were very, very few times he had a bad day. He knew how to move so quickly from what could be a really rotten day to a better place. His temperament and his spirit never flexed.

My dad lived a full and rich life.

And his favorite phrase that captured a life well-lived …
"This is livin'!"

(If you're reading this and you knew my dad, can't you just hear him saying those words? Oh, how I miss him.)
It seems so appropriate, and honoring, to tell you a bit about my dad before I give you a peek into how I'm trying to follow his example. You'll meet him in a couple pages.

I hope you find hope and a little laughter in the celebrations and messes I'm sharing. You'll also find a few pages in here where I've simply recorded fun moments, and scratch-your-head moments. Events that still make me giggle and help create my full life.

Maybe you'll see a few of your stories in some of my stories.

Life is good.
Gaye Lindfors
St. Paul, Minnesota
December 5, 2016

P.S. Sometimes, I use fancy phrases and words like "Good grief!" and "Wow!" and "Ooftah!," along with other very impressive, exceptional-writer-words. "Ooftah" is my favorite word. I think it's the perfect word, because it can mean whatever I need it to mean. My friend, Nancy Jacobsen, often reminds me that I'm spelling it wrong. It is supposed to be "Uff da." And you know? I just can't get into the rhythm of spelling it correctly. So, I'm asking forgiveness right up front for messing up this beautiful little word, with a big hug to Nancy for trying to keep me true to my Norwegian roots.

This is Livin'! My Dad

It's how my dad lived his life …
Creating *"This is livin'!"* moments.

I don't think I ever heard dad complain. About anything.
And I know I never heard him say a bad word about anyone. Ever.
He was too busy looking for the good.

What an awe-inspiring way to live.

Dad loved life. Profoundly. Deeply. Loving life came from his soul—it was who he was.

He found joy in the little things …
A tasty slice of pumpkin pie.
A good (very weak) cup of coffee.
Fishing with the grandkids.
Eating vanilla ice cream while watching the Minnesota Vikings on TV.
Listening to the Twins baseball game on the radio while reading the paper.
Talking with his students about farming and what it means to be a good citizen.
Prayer breakfasts in Fertile, Minnesota on Saturday mornings.

He'd smile his crooked smile with a dimple in only one cheek, shake his head, and exclaim with the same excitement and bright eyes as a child opening his first Christmas present … ***"This is livin'!"***

I often wondered how he stayed so positive. How he always saw the good in every situation and in every person he met. Always ready with a good word.

I think I've figured it out.

Dad's priorities were clear: faith in God, family, friends, farming, and living in service to others. He didn't want to waste a second as he lived in those what-really-matters moments. He saw so much good around him—why waste energy on things that might steal his joy?

It wasn't that he lived in a fairytale world. Good heavens—No. He and mom faced some extremely tough challenges and heart-breaking tragedies. But dad didn't let those events define him, or define his day.

He knew the messy moments were temporary ... not a place to put down roots. My wise, faith-filled father knew that if he kept his eyes on Jesus, his heart, soul, and emotions would find their way back to joy and hope—a happy place.

Even during the sad times, dad knew there was still something good happening around him. He had the ability to see the one little streak of sunshine trying to break through the storm clouds. He reached for it and hung on.

Dad didn't wait for life to be perfect before he started enjoying it. He created his life by filling it with good things. And he looked for the good things that others brought into it.

He created a rich life …
Looking for and celebrating the good moments, experiences, and amazing people in his life.
Discovering how to work through the difficult situations by leaning into God's promises.
Learning how to move from messy moments to happy places.

I want to live like that.
Every day.
In honor of my dad.

"This is Livin'!"
What a great way to experience life.

Gaye's Observations on Learning to Live a Great Life

I Almost Missed the Conversation

"Girl, you really need to clean that out."

The young man offering this undisputed advice was right. My billfold was stuffed, and the zipper was caught on a corner of a receipt crammed in with the bills, scratch paper, dirty pennies, and cellophane-wrapped toothpicks.

I bet his billfold was crisply organized, with no slips of paper spilling out. He certainly appeared more put together than me.

I had gone into the Verizon store with a headache and a cell phone that wouldn't send text messages. Upon entering this land of gadgets, the staff had introduced me (with a bit of fanfare) to Brett, the young store manager. Everything about him looked … perfect. Everything about me looked … not perfect.

Brett was wearing a silk vest under his snappy suit, and his shoes were so shiny that I could see the reflection of my blue canvas Sketchers in them. His pants were creased, he didn't have a hair out of place, and everything about his look said, "confidence." My attire testified to my harriedness and to that silent prayer going through my head …

"Oh please, Lord, don't let me run into anyone I know today."

I was disheveled and unkempt. My hair hadn't seen shampoo, Velcro rollers, or the curling iron for days. I was hoping I'd remembered to change out of my "wear these only at home" pants.

Marching into the store, my attitude almost dared anyone to take too much of my time. My focus was written on the inside of my eyeballs: get the phone fixed, and get out. I wasn't interested in chit chat. And no, I didn't have time to take a survey.

Just as I was moving into my "Let's get this done so I can move on to the rest of my list of things to do today" focus, Brett sheepishly approached me and said, "I really don't know a lot about phones. They hired me to help fix the people problems, to turn things around. And you can guess what that means. I'm not always the most liked person who works here."

Well, if that didn't change my perspective on this store visit. Bells and whistles and sirens started going off in my head as I considered what it must feel like for him to work there. He's not a techie. He's a walking fashion statement—a 3-piece suit among the trendy casual. And he was brought in to fix the store's people problems. God bless him.

Under that sharp attire, spiffy look, and hair that had received a whole lot of attention, was a heart feeling insecure, friendless, and overwhelmed.

Lord, show me what my new friend, Brett, needs this morning.

While Brett checked my phone settings, got me a new SIM card, and reviewed the access availability in the area where I lived, we talked about the challenges of working with people. We also discussed John Deere and Massey Ferguson tractors, the uniqueness of growing up in Small Town, USA, and the joy of grandparents. All the while, he tapped on his hair to make sure it was still in place.

As it turned out, this Verizon visit wasn't about getting my phone fixed. It was about two people making a human connection. Brett needed a friendly conversation with someone who wouldn't argue with him or leave him out of the conversation because he was "the boss." I needed a reminder that life is bigger and more important than my schedule, and my time, and my phone.

People matter.
Hearts matter.
God placing us right where He wants us to be matters.

As I struggled to get my driver's license out of my bursting-at-the-seams billfold, Brett's comment made me smile. His words felt comfortable. Friendly.

We shared a little break from what was hassling us for 20 minutes. He'd been encouraged, I had gotten my phone fixed, and we both had laughed. It was a DIVINE appointment.

And I had almost missed the conversation.

She's in Charge

She was "The One in Charge of All Things Important."

She relished her role. And I found it … annoying.

Mom and I were heading into the eye doctor's office for an exam. But first, we had one clear focus … one mission … one intention. Get mom to the bathroom for bladder relief. NOW.

I knew where the bathroom was, and we were moving fast. But then we scurried past the little sign in front of the receptionist's desk that said, "Please wait here until someone can assist you."

The One in Charge of All Things Important sternly declared, *"Stop! You must wait until we ask you to come forward."*

Well. She might as well have been speaking to the wall of fancy glass frames. She was not going to slow mom down. Mom had urgent business to take care of.

We continued our speedy advance with mom's gray hairs blowing back from her face, and her eyes focused on the door that said, "Women." I turned back to The One in Charge of All Things Important and replied, *"We are just going to the bathroom."*

Good grief. You would have thought we were going to steal state medical secrets or were involved in a plot to take down the entire optometric industry.

The exchange lasted maybe ten seconds. A really small slice of time in the big picture of life. But the attitude of The One in Charge of All Things Important continued to annoy me for hours after mom's eye appointment.

I found The One in Charge of All Things Important irritating. Insensitive. Bossy. Unaware. And much too self-important.

And then I had one of those moments of self-reflection. You know, one of those moments when you realize that it's *your own* response that is a bit out of perspective. For Pete's sake. This ten second messy moment was not a big deal!

Time for a reset. I needed to change my perspective.

Perhaps The One in Charge of All Things Important was very stressed out. It's possible that she'd had too many experiences with people who ignored her, dismissed her desire for an orderly and efficient office, and she had decided she was just done being pushed around.

I decided to be grateful that the bathroom wasn't at the *end* of the hallway.

I get myself so annoyed sometimes by things that don't really matter. In the big scheme of things, in a life that is really short, in a world filled with blessings and laughter and sunshine, I need to let my annoyances go.

So, I'm not going to let silly situations be in charge of my peace of mind.

Life will be better then. I'm staying in my happy place.

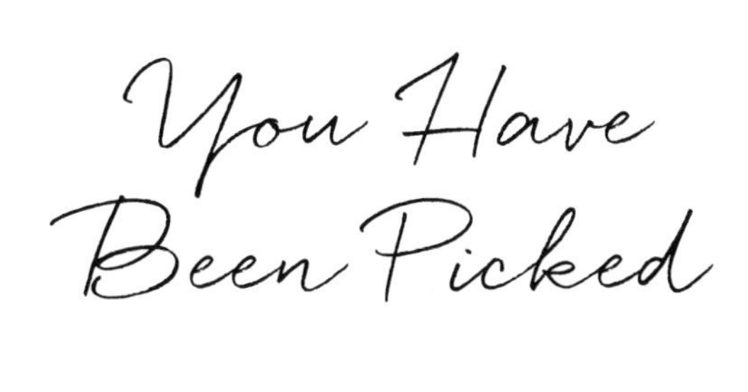

The apprehension shows up in those early years when friends are made and teams are formed—THE FEAR OF NOT BEING PICKED.

The awareness that someone has the power and influence to suggest "You don't measure up" puts a knot in our stomachs even as we're learning to read from the Dick and Jane book and tie our own shoes.
Kick-ball teams.
Birthday parties.
Junior choir solos.

This fear takes on a life of its own as we move through years when so much of how we view ourselves is determined by others.
Competitions.
Cliques.
Sports teams.
School dances.
Scholarships.
Selection committees.

Don't you wish we'd just grow out of this fear? That we'd learn our lessons early and then, never ever worry again about not being selected?

It just doesn't work that way. And, that's an Ooftah.
Someone else gets the promotion.
You don't make the team.
The "no thank you" email arrives from the hiring company.
You get laid off.
The invitation doesn't arrive.
Your phone doesn't ring.

It's all part of this "dance of life."
Sometimes, we are selected.
Sometimes, we aren't.

So, yes. Our lives will have moments that may disappoint us, because it's hard to not be picked.
We are disappointed not only because we wanted to go, attend, be the favorite, be the best, but also because not being picked may be a sign that we just don't measure up, and we take that fear to a whole new level.

It's not that we didn't get the job. It is that we believe we aren't good enough for any job.
It's not that we didn't get invited to the party. It is that we believe no one ever wants to be around us.
It's not that we didn't receive the award. It is that we believe people would laugh if they knew we hoped for it.

So how about this ...
Instead of taking our disappointing moments to the extreme levels of hopelessness which is incorrect thinking and just makes us feel worse, let's remember all the times we ARE picked.

We get on the team.
We are invited.
We secure the job.
We receive the card in the mail.
Those good things happen, too, you know!

Don't forget the good times.

If it helps, note the "you are picked" moment and write it down on a sticky post-it note. Slap it on your bathroom mirror.
Take a picture of the high-five letter and make it your phone screen saver.
Tell your friend about your cool moment and let her become your personal PR rep.

And then, let's remember the picking that matters most.

> *"I have chosen you and have not rejected you.*
> *So do not fear, for I am with you;*
> *Do not be dismayed, for I am your God.*
> *I will strengthen you and help you;*
> *I will uphold you with my righteous right hand."*
> *(Isaiah 41:9-10)*

You have been picked.

The King of Kings always chooses YOU.

The last runner brought the tears and the clarity.

Sitting at a stoplight, I watched a group of high school track guys cross the street in front of me. A little pack of lean, toned athletes. Then a few moments later, just as the light changed to green, one lone, lanky runner pulling up the rear stopped on the corner, distancing himself even more from the group.

The tears began rolling down my cheeks. My heart ached for him as he put one hand on a knee and the other on the stoplight pole, gasping to catch his breath, trying to keep upright.

I wanted to yell out the window, *"Keep going! You're doing great!"* Instead, I whispered, *"Hang in there. You're better than you think you are right now."*

My tears caught me off-guard.

I wondered about that as I drove down the street. I thought about how emotional I'd been feeling about little things, things where my impatience, cynicism, or curt responses seemed way out of proportion to the situation. Moments when I felt like a sponge, soaking up all the heartache and sadness that I perceived my friends were feeling.

What had I done when the exasperation and those emotions came? I just kept moving … Going. Doing. Fixing. Working harder and faster. At the same time, there were fewer hours of sleep on my agenda. More sugar and fewer veggies. Less sunlight.

I saw myself in that runner, trying hard to keep up, seeing everyone else get ahead faster, feeling like I was left out and always behind. But my body just didn't have what it needed to keep functioning at my very best.

Then, the clarity came. The real life stuff that was messing with my happy place was not a list of really big deals. There was nothing going on that created a crisis or required a major decision or was anything to get too worked up about. There was nothing to fix. My body was just tired. And hungry. And thirsty.

I had forgotten that, sometimes, working harder and faster and crazier doesn't fix everything. Sometimes, I need to grab a handful of carrots. Go for a walk. Drink two big glasses of water.

Sometimes, I just need to rest.

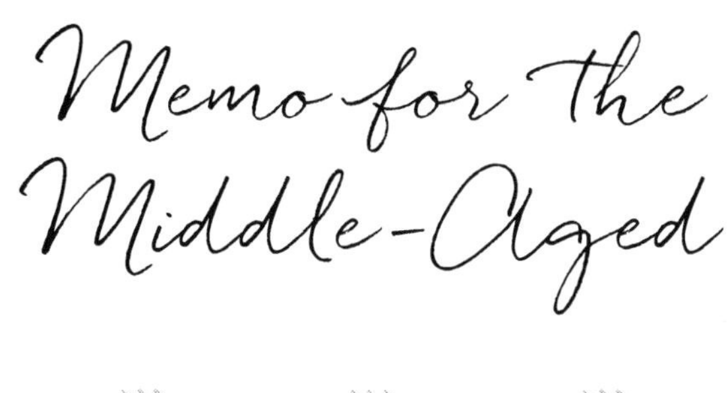

Over spaghetti and meat sauce, I'm trying to explain to Steve what I think the lines along the sides of my lips and chin remind me of.

Like the face of a puppet … no … marionette … no …
Like the face on a ventriloquist's dummy.
Yes! That's it.

The look on his face tells me he thinks this may be a trick question, and that he needs to think carefully about his response.

These lines of wrinkles that start at the corners of my lips and crease alongside my chin are relatively new, I think. And they don't appear to be features that are easily removed or covered up.

Sigh.

If only I had …

Those of you who remember Bobby Sherman, the Bee Gees, manual or electric typewriters, 8-track tapes, homes without dishwashers, and never-wear-jeans-to-church rules …

We're entering, or have entered, that chapter in life when earlier decisions haunt us. At the same time, we might start to believe our ability to transform lives and make a difference is held back by age, health, or the "too late" syndrome.

Fill in the blank:
If only I had ________________________ …

… Used more moisturizer. Stayed out of the sun. Finished that degree. Saved more money. Traveled more. Eaten better. Stood up to my boss. Been nicer to my parents. Taken more chances.

Good grief.

Social media has told me about younger women doing really amazing things. They are planting community gardens in South Africa, writing beautiful blog posts that transform into messages of Hope and Meaning, and sporting casual and trendy outfits that we know were just "thrown together."

As impressed as I am with their contributions, their efforts make me feel … insignificant. When I let myself enter the world of comparisons, my service for the women's group seems so small; my words sound out of touch and irrelevant; I don't have the interest or the know-how to be "casual and trendy."

If only I had (fill in the blank) ____________________; before now; NOW it's too late.

I know I'm not the only one who has peered into this window of doubt and disappointment. It can throw us into a downward spiral of thinking *"Why bother?"* Then, we eat unhealthy amounts of ice cream and stop trying.

So, let's just STOP.
Just stop this kind of nonsense thinking, shall we?

Today. Right now.

This kind of thinking, whining, and pity-party planning is more than just comparative-itis (which we know should be banished from our minds and emotions forever). This is about downplaying and disrespecting our experiences from years past. This is about beating ourselves up for decisions we made when we were young and clueless, and when we just plain needed to grow up. This is about believing that age makes us irrelevant, that it's too late to dream, that it's too late to make a difference.

Who says? I mean, really. Who says?

Your life, just as it is today, matters.

Yes, you made decisions in the past that you wish you could do over.

Yes, your body is changing, and health really does keep you from doing some activities. But it doesn't keep you from doing *something.*

Your home and your relationships may feel tired and empty.
So be the first to reach out and reconnect. Be the influencer of good instead of supporting the disconnect with your silence.
Don't give in, and don't give up.
DO SOMETHING.

How about if we start by choosing LIFE, life in all its faith-filled and fun-filled fullness? Choose to encourage the timid, help the weak, be patient with everyone, love our neighbors, and be kind.

That, dear friends, is what will make a difference. This attitude has nothing to do with age.

My life has been more greatly influenced and affected by the little things, words, and actions of people around me than by any big cause or accomplishment. And the impact was never defined by the age of the person who was loving me, encouraging me, and celebrating me.

Let's bring the little things back into our world and the worlds of those around us, and continue to make a difference.

Instead of *"If only I had ..."*
We will say, *"Because I did."*

This, my friend, is livin'.

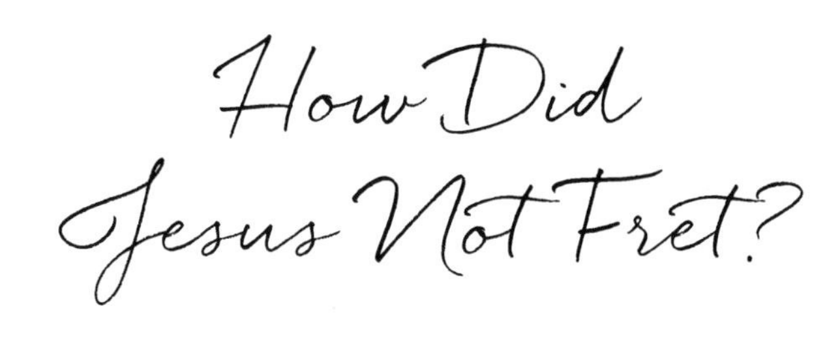

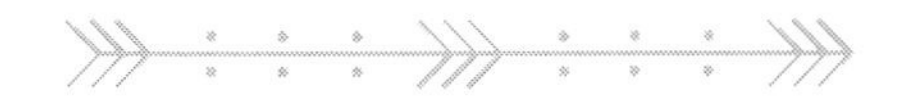

Good morning, Lord.
It's me again.

Since you and I have this agreement that we will have truthful conversations with each other, can I just say …

All I want to do today is fret.

Did you ever have a day like that, Lord? A day when fretting just seemed to be the appropriate response to life? Yeah. I bet you did.

But I also know you didn't do the fretting.

How did you manage that? That whole not fretting thing?

I mean, really. I'm trying to picture what that might have looked like … You walking on the shores of Galilee in your sandals, fretting. Wringing your hands in worry about not having enough fish for everybody to eat. Whining about the people you work with—disciples who couldn't get their acts together, especially Peter who just wouldn't stop talking. I can't imagine you hiding under the burlap covers wishing you could stay in bed all day because the next 12 hours just seemed to be filled with too much responsibility.

That just doesn't compute.

You never fretted. You never lost your cool, except for that righteous anger time when you flipped the tables over in the temple. I don't think you were calm that day, but it wasn't a fretting lack of calmness.

And you know, I don't think your "I'm not fretting today" decision ever had anything to do with willpower or resolutions or just going to the happy place in your head.

We learn that from your friends who knew you, those who wrote down what they observed.

*Your close friend, Mark, wrote, "Very early in the morning, while it was still dark, Jesus got up, left the house and **went off to a solitary place, where he prayed**." (Mark 1:35)*

*Dr. Luke tells us that "Jesus often **withdrew to lonely places and prayed**." (Luke 5:16)*

I guess you chose not to focus on your list of things to fret about. You focused on your Father, instead.

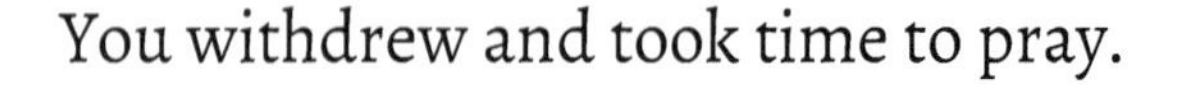

Rather than looking at all the messy moments that could make you miserable on earth, you looked to The One who knew exactly what you needed and who would then give those things to you ... Direction. Love. Hope. Reassurance. Companionship.

So, Lord.
Lesson learned. Or should I say, lesson reminded.
Let's start this day over again ...

Good morning, Lord.
It's me again.

Thank you for giving me the peace that replaces my fretting.
Let's do life together today.

Playing the Game

I am not an athlete. As much as I would love to have the long legs, arm reach, or muscle strength of an athlete, I am short with jiggly thighs and limited upper body strength.

Growing up, I remember running in a track meet. (Yes, I know. Short with jiggly thighs doesn't create an inspiring athlete-in-motion visual. But in my small hometown of Climax, Minnesota, almost everybody had to participate on the teams in order to organize any type of sports. So I ran track.) After one particular regional meet, the school's newsletter noted that I came in third in the 400-meter run. Impressive ... if you had no idea that there were only three of us who raced.

An athlete? No. But I loved athletics. And I really loved girls' basketball.

Here again, basketball teams generally didn't recruit for short and jiggly talent. But I was a warm body who wanted to play.

As I look back at those basketball games, I remember what I loved most—the camaraderie, the bus rides, the high-fives, the warm-up music, the cheering. But I did not like the ill-fitting shorts we had to wear. And I didn't like actually playing the game. Most of the time when I was on the court, I was silently praying my teammates would not throw me the ball. I wanted to be there, moving around, anticipating the play, but please, please, please do not give me the ball. Strange, I know.

The problem was in my head. I was afraid that I would not know what to do with the ball when it was in my hands. Desperately fearful of messing up and making a mistake, it was easier for me to not get the ball than to face the humiliation of doing something wrong with it when I got it. Part of the problem was not wanting to take the risk, but the bigger problem was not believing I was good enough to play.

Maybe my fear was also a reaction to one of my mom's stories, one that I have heard for 50+ years. In one of her first high school basketball games, a teammate passed her the ball. Mom dribbled down the court. Set a perfect layup. Swoosh ...and landed the ball into the other team's basket. Mortified and humiliated cannot adequately describe how horrible she felt. I feel that pain every time I hear the play-by-play.

But back to my point.
I believe that when we look back at our younger selves, and then look at our adult selves, we see behaviors and thinking patterns that have remained with us. Only the scenarios have changed.

Just as I was afraid to take the ball and do something with it on the court, I'm sometimes afraid to step out into a bigger challenge when an opportunity is tossed my way.

When the idea of stepping into a larger speaking platform appears, I pause. *"What if I'm not good enough?"* When the invitation comes for a radio show, I pause. *"What if I'm not as good as they think I am?"* When it's my turn to cook a meal, I pause. *"What if someone dies from eating it?"* (Really! That runs through my mind.)

Now may I just mention here, except for that whole cooking struggle ... I know I am capable of doing these bigger things when the opportunities are presented. But oh, the fear that rises up in my throat too instinctively! That fear rides on my shoulders, yelling the what-if's into my ear louder than the you-can-do-this encouragements coming from the cheerleaders on the sidelines. So I pause.

Pausing is my safe place. And in that safe place, I convince myself that my hesitation is smart. I listen to the self-doubt. I tune my ears to the fear.

And the opportunities are lost.

So, before I get to that place, I need to reset my thinking. And then, step up and do what scares me without worrying about guaranteed perfection.

My dad loved watching girls' basketball games. He was so proud of us—in all our very not-athletic attempts to play the game. He especially loved watching the scrappy players, those who fought hard for the ball and didn't care if the shots or the blocks weren't pretty. The players who showed up and played with guts and heart.

I want to be that scrappy player and stop trying to be the perfect player. I want to knock fear off my shoulders and send it to the locker room to shower.

Swoosh! That's what I want.

I want to play.
I want the ball.

What's the Plan?

"What's the plan?"

This is my mom's favorite question. She asks it during the middle-of-the-night wake-ups, first thing in the morning, and several times throughout the daily routine. And it always makes me chuckle. With her short-term memory challenges, I know she's not going to remember my response for more than a few moments. And yet, she asks, *"What's the plan?"* And I respond.

It takes me back to summer days, long ago.

Every morning of summer vacation, my sisters and I would begin the day sitting on the red, plastic upholstered kitchen chairs arranged around the shiny, silver Formica table with the aluminum edging. Mom would help us make a list—our plan for the day.

This plan always included work responsibilities. Shell the peas. Mow the lawn. Clean the junk drawer. Wash the slab. I got tired just making the list and wondered why we had to have a plan and why the slab had to be hosed down because the big red two-ton truck was just going to get it muddy again, anyway.

There was ALWAYS a plan.

I don't mind answering mom's favorite question these days. Her world has gotten pretty small, and there aren't a lot of activities to plan for her day. What she's really asking is, *"When are you leaving? Who's coming to stay?"*

Today, these short conversations with her prompt me to think more deeply about the question.

*What **is** the plan?*

"Caregiver" is a new role—staying with mom for companionship, as a jigsaw puzzle partner, and for providing reminders, like short-term memory joggers. Julie and Lori and I are still trying to figure out the plan. Each sister is creating a new normal for our lives as we take turns using the card table in the extra bedroom as a place to get our work done, joining mom for walks, and sleeping in the trundle bed at night.

We love our mom.

But what's the plan?

This is a new chapter in life, and I didn't foresee the storyline unfolding in this direction. Who does? When you're a little girl, sitting cross-legged on the kitchen floor with the blue bowl tucked in your lap to capture the peas you're shelling, you don't imagine that one day your helping hands will be needed to take care of your mom around the clock.

How do we children do this? What happens next?
And then I remember.

There is a plan.
There always is.
God has it.

This "I didn't see it coming story-changer" I'm experiencing isn't a surprise to God. He's not at all confused by it, wringing His hands and worrying about what this means for us. He's not trying to figure out what to do next.

God KNOWS the plan.

And because I know that He is smack-dab in the middle of this chapter with us, I trust the story, even if I don't know what the next chapter looks like.

These days my sisters and I are not shelling peas or weeding the garden or cleaning cupboards or washing the slab.

We're listening to and telling stories from long ago, making oatmeal, watching Charles Stanley sermons, laughing a lot, going on drives, making sure pills are taken and lunch is eaten, and figuring out the crosswords …

And answering the question, *"What's the plan?"*
Hey. We're working it out, Mom.
One day at a time … grateful, so grateful, for these moments.

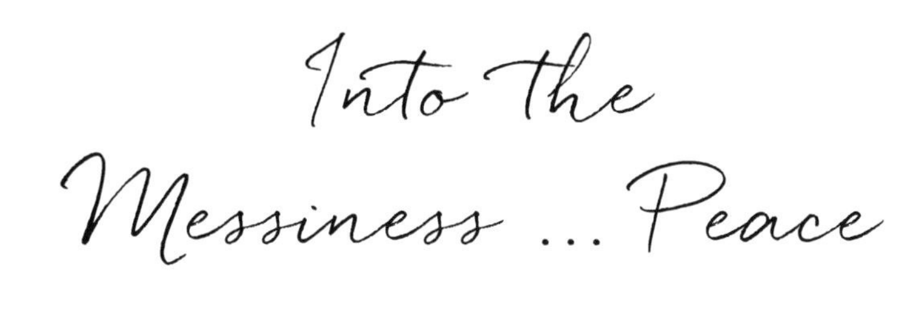

Into the Messiness ... Peace

There was nothing remotely fancy about the place of Jesus' birth.

Stables are never voted "Cleanest place in the world to have a baby." Wet, dirty straw. Snorting cattle and braying donkeys. No turned-down sheets on a bed; no little chocolate mint on the pillow. And you have to believe that Mary and Joseph would have loved a good, hot shower after a long, dusty, dirty road trip.

Seems rather messy, doesn't it?

It was into this messiness that Jesus came.

Overnights in stables may not be part of our lives. But messiness certainly is. A medical diagnosis, strained or broken relationships, unemployment, forgetful parents, or a schedule that runs us ragged.

It is into this messiness that Jesus comes.

Hope comes with Christmas. Messiness happens, and life can sometimes feel tough. But it is the birth of this baby Jesus that brings Hope, and Peace, and Comfort into every single moment, no matter how messy the moment.

> *"Peace I leave with you; my peace I give you. I do not give to you as the world gives. Do not let your hearts be troubled and do not be afraid." (John 14:27)*

What a promise. Jesus meets us, right where we are.
And when He meets us, Jesus brings us Peace.

What a wonderful Christmas gift.

Peter Gives Me Hope

There are some days and weeks when I'm more grateful than usual that God doesn't expect me to be perfect to receive His love. That I don't have to have it all together before He can use me to encourage, support, or walk with my friends through life's frustrations.

When I think about this, I think about Peter and smile. You gotta' love the guy.

He was one of the 12 people Jesus chose to be in His inner circle. Disciples. World-changers. A pretty cool group to be a part of, right?

Peter. So passionate. Expressive. Emotional. Definitely not perfect. Not proper. Not a pretty package tied up with a pretty bow kind-of-guy who has life all figured out. Peter speaks before he thinks; acts before he considers.

My image of Peter is one of a guy filled with words and bluster. I picture his face frequently looking bright red because he's a fisherman, which means he's in the sun a lot, and he's always talking fast and intensely, making a point. He wants to be in on everything; always, he wants to know what's going on.

I think Peter might also be a bit out-of-shape. Check this out …

"So Peter and the other disciple started for the tomb. Both were running, but the other disciple outran Peter and reached the tomb first." (John 20:3-4)

(It's interesting that this foot race was even mentioned. And even more interesting? The writer of those words, John, was "the other disciple" who got there first. I wonder if John wanted to make the point that he beat Peter to the tomb, but he used third person words so he wouldn't sound too cocky.)

Peter probably arrived at the tomb huffing and puffing. One hand leaning on the stone and the other on his knee, bending over to get the stitch out of his side. And when he realized that there was a big story associated with this empty tomb, he wanted to be the one to tell it ... once he caught his breath.

Peter is a study in contrasts, isn't he? He defended Jesus, slicing off the right ear of one of the men who came to take Jesus away to be killed. Yet hours later, he denied knowing Jesus and abandoned Him when events got rough and dangerous.

And then. After the story of the tomb unfolded and the resurrection was accomplished, Peter is asked three times by Jesus if he loves Him. This is a chance for Peter to move beyond his past denials and guilt, to make things right. He responds, "Yes." And all of Peter's passion and commitment and desire to be who God wants him to be comes alive.

I get this. I understand Peter's behavior.

Impulsiveness is part of my story, too.
I sometimes speak before I think and act before I consider. *"I'm sorry"* is a required response too many times. My life's not a pretty package tied up with a pretty bow, either.

I read about Peter, and I raise my hand and say, *"Me, too."*

Peter didn't have his act together.
Jesus knew that.
He called Peter anyway.

I don't have my act together.
Jesus knows that.
He calls me anyway.

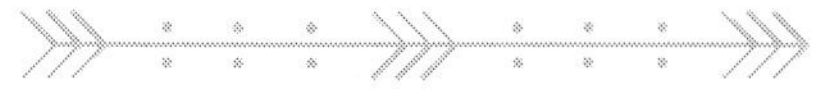

"Really, lady? You think this is a good idea?"

The teenager supervising the trampolines was probably weighing his options—just call 911 right away or wait it out for the stories he could tell.

Our little group was at SkyZone. You know. The trampoline warehouse that reminds us our bodies aren't what they used to be. The place where women of 50+ years come to live on the edge and, hopefully, leave without a stretcher.

I gotta' tell you. Trusting a stretch of flexible rubber to bounce you into the air and catch you when you drop to earth will motivate you to remember memorized scripture verses from years gone by really, really quickly.

For the first 30 seconds of our bouncing time, I didn't dare let my feet leave the trampoline. I weaved and bobbed as if I were trying to avoid a knock-out punch. Not a pretty picture. I felt like a tug boat riding the waves in a hurricane. When I finally let myself go, I was convinced the rubber would tear when I landed, and I'd slam into the cement floor.

And yet, all of this emotion and fear was framed by hysterical laughter. This fun-filled excursion was part of a girls' weekend with my sisters and nieces. "Living summer" we called it. Taking a break from to-do lists and heavy responsibilities and too much inside time.

Using our Groupons, we experienced kayaking without drowning. (Getting into a very narrow boat had me convinced I would end up upside down under water, kissing the sunfish.) We segway'd around the lakes and had a picnic lunch. And we stayed up late at my sister's, eating Special-K bars and watching TV re-runs.

Mom came along for the two-day party. My nephew, Scottie, was her butler, waiter, personal attendant, and chauffeur when she wasn't with us—making sure she could observe as much of the fun as possible.

Many times during our weekend fun, one of us would exclaim, *"This is livin'!"* And we'd all smile. It was THE BEST EVER EXPERIENCE.

So, having this hilariously fun and freeing weekend begs the question: Why do I put fun at the bottom of every list I write? Why do I spend too much time in "responsibility" mode? How come I always have too much to do … Work, house projects, cleaning, errands, family needs, yard work, and more work? You know what I'm talking about, right?

Oh, I'm so glad I moved the busy stuff to "least important stuff" for a few days. This weekend made me feel younger, less stressed, grateful. And nothing—Not. One. Thing.—beats laughing with my sisters.

Take it from the "Master of Assuming Responsibility and Following-through" (that's me), there will never be an ideal time to take a break. So, just create the time. Whether it's two days, an afternoon, or an hour. Just take the break.

We were made to work.
AND ...
We were made to have fun.

Let's create *This is livin'!* moments.

Let the Muffins Go

I do not claim to be a cook. Nor a baker. Nor a candlestick maker.

Kitchen and craft activities make my heart race and my palms sweat. I don't remember a time when cooking ever seemed "fun." So when I found my family's evaluation of my junior high muffin baking assignment, I smiled ... with renewed trepidation.

It was an assignment that made me wish I had taken shop classes instead of Home Economics. (Remember those days?) But back then, the classes were usually divided quite clearly between Shop for the boys and Home Ec for the girls. Good grief.

After baking our muffins, we needed to have them taste-tested and evaluated. I figured my family would be gracious. You judge …

My Mom: *"Delicious! They beat the ones she made from powdered milk!! Home Ec has really helped her."*

Julie: (The Home Ec major in college): *"Good."*

Lori: *"They were good with lots of butter."*

My Dad: *"Excellent. Moist (Is that good?). The crusts were just the way I like them."*

So many ways to read these comments, right?

We can't be good at everything. But we can be good at something. Choose your something.

Let the muffins go.

My Heart Still Wears a Parka

Winter is over in Minnesota. Can I hear an *"Amen?"* (At least we hope it is. Let's knock on wood that's no longer covered with snow, shall we?)

The thick "Michelin-man (woman)" parkas are stuffed into basement closets, stocking caps with the cute ear flaps are shoved into Tupperware organizers, and our boots … well, they're still in reachable distance because we now have this the-snow-has-melted-where-does-the-water-go thing going on.

We are pros at knowing how to protect our skin and bones during the season of blizzards and white-outs and frigid temperatures. We are survivors!

There's something else I'm good at protecting … my heart. And I don't mean from the icy snow.

There are seasons in my life when I keep a little parka wrapped around this tough and tender muscle, even when there's no threat of below zero wind chill. The heart-shaped parka is slipped on when I'm feeling a bit insecure, or tired, or overwhelmed. Part of the protection keeps other distractions from adding more weight to a heart that's already a little heavy. This makes sense. But part of the protection keeps others from seeing too much of my heart's insecurity, or weariness, or overwhelm. This doesn't make sense.

We talk so much about encouraging each other. Supporting each other. Being there for each other. We would do almost anything to help a girlfriend walk through a tough time, right?

So, why don't we let our girlfriends be there for us? Why do we think we have to be stronger, tougher, braver? **Why do we work so hard at protecting our hearts, making it impossible for others to step in and encourage and support us?**

I think many of us have compiled a list of reasons why we're afraid to let someone peek into our heavy hearts—fear of rejection and judgment, it may signal weakness, people may think less of us, etc. These *"reasons" are usually unfounded fears*. Ooftah.

I'm learning to remove some of the heart parka I wear, to let my girlfriends slip on my shoes to walk a mile with me, encourage, and laugh with me. It makes all the difference in the journey.

What about you? Wouldn't it feel good to remove your heart parka for a bit? Wouldn't it feel good to let a trusted girlfriend know that, *"Yeah, life is tough right now."* Wouldn't it feel good to have someone walk with you for a few steps?

Winter is only a season, and parkas eventually need to be taken off, boxed up, and stored in the basement.

We aren't meant to walk alone.
Our hearts are meant to be shared.

This is our season to remove our parkas.

My dream job? Private Eye.
My detective agency would be called, “It’s Sweeter When They Sweat.”

My female PI role model? Nancy Drew. That teenage amateur sleuth with friends named Beth and George and a boyfriend named Ned. I see myself as a modern-day version of Nancy. (And that’s pretty silly all by itself, because I would never consider myself a modern-day girl by any stretch of the imagination.)

But back to my dream career …

I’d be a walking fashion statement for female PI’s.
High heels. (Make that stiletto heels.)
Jeans. (Make that skinny jeans.)
Short-sleeved v-neck t-shirt. (Make that a form-fitting v-neck t-shirt.)
With a leather jacket. (Make that a waist-length leather jacket that I can actually zip up.)

I’d carry the flashlight between my teeth, run after people doing bad things, and never be out of breath.

Yup. In my dreams, I’d be one stylin’ gum-shoe.

In my reality …
I can't imagine breaking and entering.
Or being on a stake-out at night, alone.
Or talking back to some big someone threatening me with bodily harm or disfigurement.

So this whole Nancy Drew / detective agency idea probably isn't going to take off very fast. But I am discovering that my investigative juices are finding their outlet in another very special way—as part of my faith journey.

I want to know more about this big, loving, caring, Almighty God.

I desire to dig deeper. Ask serious questions. Study. Talk to people. Listen for clues about what it really means to "walk with God."

I want to be bold. To go places in my investigations where I've never gone before. Take my tools of the trade and look for fingerprints of saints who've left their mark in word, action, and blood. Study their reports. Follow their example. Analyze the clues. Study to know truth.

And just think, I can do this in slippers instead of heels and head-turning trappings. My cozy chair is the perfect investigative perch.

As I study, I will be the one sweating. Discovering where

I'm missing the mark. Being challenged to stretch and grow. Moving outside my safe-faith comfort zone.

Any good PI needs to continually check her assumptions. WHAT needs to change in my life? HOW do I change? What saddens God's heart versus what brings Him honor and praise? These answers will result in a deeper relationship with Jesus.

Yes. My investigation confirms …

Life gets sweeter when I sweat.

I was out of sorts. Uncomfortable with the attention. Self-conscious in my white tights.

I was 13 years old, standing on the stage in a college auditorium, along with eight other 4-H'ers from northern Minnesota.

We were competing in a "Good Grooming Contest." Yes, you read that correctly. A Good Grooming Contest. (Good grief. As if it's not *awkward enough* just to *be* 13 years old.)

There must have been more to that evening's event than this contest. But I have no memory of the rest of the program and the picture of us standing side-by-side on stage is seared into my brain.

Representing the Lucky Leaf 4-H Club was a treat. I loved our Club and my 4-H friends who were also my school mates, team mates, church friends, and best friends. (Small town, remember?) On this evening, my appearance, cleanliness, and "good grooming" were being evaluated by a man and a woman who, I guess, knew a lot about good grooming. The nine of us stood in what we hoped was perfect posture in a line on the stage while they threaded their way between us, looking closely at our grooming, while our parents anxiously watched from their red velvet auditorium seats.

(Really? I mean, really. Why?)

But something was definitely off for me. I just couldn't get my tights to feel right.

My pink and white dress with the thin, pink ribbon at the neckline, its Peter Pan collar, and my black patent shoes were just "too cute." My short little blond bob represented a good hair day. And I was clean.

But my white tights? Twisted. I kept squirming, pulling at them, trying to get them to straighten out. This was not the way you typically would want to stand out in a Good Grooming Contest.

Well, there wasn't any #1 Good Groomer purple ribbon in my lap on the way home. But I did eventually discover the reason for my discomfort.

One of the legs of my tights was sewn on backwards. And since my feet both point in the same direction, these tights would never have fit right. No matter how hard I squirmed.

A metaphor for life.

Sometimes you just know something's off, right? And all the wriggling and twisting and fussing doesn't make it better.

I've discovered that when the squirming starts, I need to pause and see what's going on in my heart. Do my own little evaluation of how well-groomed and clean it is. Often, my check-in requires forgiveness and a start-over.

My favorite path to a non-squirming life when things have

gotten messy? Praying the words of confession and request for a start-over in the song written by our friend and former pastor, Tom Gundermann—*"Forgive Me."*

Forgive me, Lord, forgive me,
For my heart has gone its way.
I ignored your Word, I ignored Your children.
Please, Lord, forgive me.

Take my hand and lead me away from sin.
Take my heart and make it new.
Take my life and make it Yours my King,
Help me dedicate my life to You.

Isn't that just beautiful? The message is simple—and powerful.

When my heart is uncomfortable and unsettled, I need to stop fussing and take the time to straighten it out.

What's keeping me from knowing your peace, God?

I need to slow down. Stop. Do a little heart check. Then confess where I've messed up, and ask God to get me and my heart back on track.
Whether it's tights or hearts …
It feels good to get things settled.
Comfortable.
Untwisted.
No "Good Groomer" judges are needed.

It was a bad day.
I mean, a REALLY bad day.

My friend, David (the one who wrote the Psalms), was having a day that makes me feel anxious just reading about it.

Here's how he described it in the 69th chapter of his book, verses 1-3:
- *The waters have come up to my neck …*
- *I sink in the miry depths where there is no foothold …*
- *The floods engulf me …*
- *I am worn out calling for help …*
- *My eyes fail …*

And then.
The biggie.

"Those who hate me without reason outnumber the hairs of my head…" (verse 4)

You've got to be kidding me! I break out in a sweat and feel nauseous if I think *one* person doesn't like me. Unless David was bald, I think that's a whole lot of people who weren't jostling to sit next to him in the harp choir or attending his poetry readings. And they apparently hated him for no good reason. Oh man. That's rough.

And yet …
(Don't you just love the word "yet"? It brings such hope!)

And yet …
David knew that God was faithful. He knew that God was The One who could get him out of that horrible place.

> *"**Rescue me** from the mire, do not let me sink;*
> ***Deliver me** from those who hate me, from the deep waters.*
> ***Do not let** the floodwaters engulf me or the depths swallow me up or the pit close its mouth over me.*
> ***Answer me,** O Lord, out of the goodness of your love; **in your great mercy turn to me."** (verses 14-16)*

And then in the 30th verse …

"I will praise God's name in song and glorify him with thanksgiving."

WOW.

If the number of people who hated me equaled the number of the hairs on my head, it would take me awhile to get to the praise part of my prayer.

I think I'd spend a lot of time fretting, wringing my hands, and whining about how unfair life is and how those people who hate me are stupid. And wrong. (The kind of explanations we used in junior high when all our insecurities seemed to emerge simultaneously, right along with an acne breakout and a pop quiz in Life Science.)

But, boy. Don't you just love David? He was having such a bad day. And yet ...
He chose to focus on The One who could bring him to a different emotional and spiritual place.
He knew how to move from his messy moment to his happy place.
He praised God and gave thanks.

May it be so in MY life.

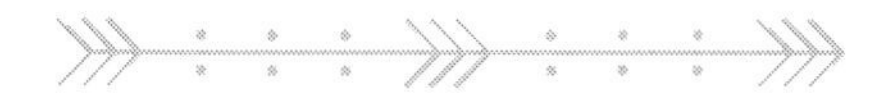

I hadn't been that uncomfortable since … well, since the girdle days.

You know. The pre-Spanx® suck-it-in and pull-it-up girdle. Made from rubber ripped off the back tires of the 1972 Ford LTD. It felt like a tourniquet around your waist and thighs. Thick, tight, hard to breath. Extremely uncomfortable.

Getting that girdle on and off required a follow-up shower and a nap. And an oxygen tank. It left me panting and sweating and worn out. The process was almost as miserable as actually wearing it. Nothing comfortable about that body wear.

I felt that same level of discomfort as I read David's note in Psalm 19.

(Who would have thought that there was a spiritual observation to be gained from putting on a girdle. Go figure. God certainly has a sense of humor.)

> *"May the words of my mouth and the meditation of my heart be pleasing in your sight, O Lord, my Rock and my Redeemer." (Psalm 19:14)*

It was the "meditation of my heart" line that brought discomfort. Big time discomfort.

Don't you sometimes want to say, *"But God, surely you don't mean that my thoughts have to please you in* ***this*** *particular circumstance? You don't understand. I am soooo angry. The other person was mean, unfair, wrong, hurtful. I have a right to be..."*

In those moments, the meditations of my heart are not pleasing in anyone's sight. I just want that mean person to be miserable.

Lord, have mercy.

My righteous indignation is most passionate when it's my friend who has been wronged. I love being a friend who stands up for those whom I care about, who sees an injustice and wants to help, and who stands up for someone who may lack the strength because she's been knocked down one too many times.

I'm also learning about the danger of letting an injustice take on a life of its own. Steal my Joy. Undermine my Peace. It's easy to become caught up in the emotions generated while defending our friends. But eventually, the injustice and our defense could become the substance of the story and the end of the story. What I focus on—meditate on—is the messiness. There is no room for positive resolution. Grace. Forgiveness. Or moving on.

God has made His point clear. In addition to being The One who can meet us in that encounter with injustice, He is to also be my focus. And my meditation must please Him. This means that it can't include bitterness or vengeance or getting-even or hateful words. Even if it's on the behalf of my friend.

So I reconcile my desire to help my friend with what God has called me to do. I will choose to stand up for her. Seek justice. Defend her. And move to a place in the messiness where my words and actions please Him. It's possible to do both.

These "old girdle" types of verses like Psalm 19 make me sweat and feel uncomfortable, yet, I'm glad the Bible includes them. How else would I grow? How else would I know who I want to become and what it takes to get there?

I'll take the old girdles made from divine words and truth. But the old girdles made from rubber that require dusting yourself with talcom powder first? No thank you. I'll pass.

Panic During the Biggest Game

Biggest Game of the Year.
I'm talking football. Super Bowl.

It was February 2, 2014. Seattle Seahawks vs the Denver Broncos, led by my favorite professional quarterback, Payton Manning.

I take my football very seriously.

My favorite part of The Biggest Game? All the pull-on-the-heart-strings background stories we hear in the 63 hours preceding the game. You know, the family vignettes, the tough-times-made-me-the-football-player-I-am-today, the passionate tributes to coaches, mentors, and parents. I absolutely love that kind of human interest, "color" reporting.

So I was kind of hoping I'd get to see some of the pre-game sentimental anecdotes on that particular Sunday afternoon.

However …
Since I spend a lot of caregiving time at my mom's, when I am at home with my husband Steve I try to be fully present. And on that Sunday—the day of The Biggest Game—I was at home. That created a dilemma. Steve doesn't share my fondness for the emotional sports stories. Spending eight hours watching TV

doesn't bring him to his Happy Place. Nor does he share my deep appreciation for football, unless it's the Minnesota Vikings.

What to do … What to do …

We compromised.
We decided that we wouldn't watch the pre-game, all-afternoon stories. We'd turn on the TV 30 minutes before the game to catch the best of the best tear-jerkers. And then, enjoy the game.

But, oh, yeah. That 30-minutes before the game time slot? It airs during the national news. In Steve's world, watching the national news is sacred routine. In my world, it's just more bad news from around the globe.

I could hear the voice of the "experts"…
Which is better? Getting your way, or honoring the relationship?
(What is their perspective? Have they ever watched the heart-warming stories before The Biggest Game?!)

So, we compromised again.
We'll turn the channel from the news early to hear the opera diva sing the national anthem while watching close-ups of the players on the sidelines gazing emotionally at the sky. (You think they're getting all emotional about patriotism and being in The Biggest Game? I think the tears are because the players are nervous, and they wish they had a few more minutes in the bathroom.)

Now, fellow-football-fans, before we get too frustrated with Steve's reluctance to fill our living room with all-day football … let me just say …
Instead of watching the lead-up to The Biggest Game, we were spending the early afternoon reading, which is one of my most

favorite ways to spend time with him. So I was happy with Plan B. It just wasn't my Plan A.

So, as agreed …
We (well, Steve in control of the remote) checked out the national news and turned it back to Channel 9 for the opera singer, the sky-gazing, and the big kick-off.

And then …
Oh. My. Word.
My world turned absolutely upside down ...

The sports announcers on Channel 9 are running the play-by-play in Spanish!
Yes, Spanish.
(I don't know Spanish.)

I'm watching my Payton Manning do something horrible in the first few seconds of the game and the fans are going crazy, but I don't understand it … because it's in Spanish!!

I bolt out of the living room chair faster than an off-side penalty. But all I can do is stand there, staring at the TV, with no clue what to do. Then I take control of the remote. Every other channel is in the language I understand, but there's no English-speaking announcer on my Channel 9.
It's. In. Spanish!

I think of calling my friend, Dan Thornberg, who taught himself to speak Spanish when we were at Bethany School of Missions 30+ years ago. But I don't even know if he likes football and oh, yeah, I don't have his phone number.

And then I see two points on the scoreboard for the opposing team that is not Payton's! How in the name of all things good like football did I miss so much in 12 seconds? And again, why isn't the announcer speaking English?

I call my sister, Julie. I'm still standing inches in front of the TV because I don't know where else one stands when she's missing The Biggest Game of the year!

Julie can't stop emoting about poor Payton and two points and a safety. But by this time I'm frantic and I just can't stop yelling ... *"But it's in Spanish! And I don't understand Spanish!"* I finally just hang up.

Meanwhile, back on the couch ...

Steve is finding this whole scenario quite humorous. Head tilted back, laughing-from-the-belly humorous.

I think about how fast I can get over to Julie's to watch the game in English. And besides, she's making homemade caramels over there.

I finally calm myself enough to take a look at the remote. I see the problem. There is this little white button with "Lang" written above it. I pressed it once. And TV announcers Joe Buck and Troy Aikman appear on my screen speaking English.

Regular breathing resumes.
The world is back in its upright position.

This is livin'.

No Distractions

I nicknamed the woman on the right "Anxious Alice." The friend who stood to her left became "Helpful Hannah."

They were standing in front of me at the Panera counter placing a very complicated bagel order. Anxious Alice desired a certain number of blueberry bagels, several cinnamon crunch, a few whole grain, a couple asiago cheese, and a few other choices. Then she began to explain to the young girl behind the counter exactly how she wanted them sliced, sorted, and bagged. She was being fastidiously particular.

At the same time, her friend Helpful Hannah was boldly trying to be … helpful. She was asking clarifying questions, interpreting Anxious Alice's requests, offering suggestions, and trying to uncomplicate the order. Unfortunately, it seemed to create more confusion and frustration for everybody.

Without warning, Anxious Alice let everyone know she had heard enough from Helpful Hannah.

Anxious Alice turned to her friend and in a very exasperated and firm tone said, *"Would you please stop talking. I can't hear what the girl behind the counter is saying when you are talking to me. You are distracting me."*

Helpful Hannah stopped talking, abruptly.

Well. That little scenario had my name all over it. The little twinge in my heart told me so.

There may be times when I am Anxious Alice, but most of the time? Just call me Helpful Hannah.

I want to help. Fix. Make the pain go away. Change the situation.

Nothing wrong with that, *until* I get in the way.
Until I become noisy and confusing. Distracting.
Until I keep my friend from hearing from The One Who Knows Best.

Those of us who wear Helpful Hannah on our name badges need to remember that we can't always make everything OK.

Sometimes we need to stop talking, stop advising, and stop fixing, and simply walk along with our friend in prayerful silence.

Let God do His best work.

Yeah. I need to remember that.

The cable was as thin as my confidence that it could actually carry my weight.

I looked across the ravine to my landing place, and then, I looked down into the ravine where I did not want my landing place to be. Then I just trembled ...

I was zip lining for the first time. Good grief.

Now just let me say, for those of you who have done this and the experience was not fearful and only exhilarating … I applaud you. High-five. Atta' Girl. I'm impressed. Really.

But my first time? This was even waaaayyy more unsettling than The Bouncy Gym. At the Bouncy Gym, I knew that when my feet left the ground they would certainly return within moments. And they had something soft to land on. But skimming across the tops of the trees meant that my feet weren't going to hit the earth for a while. And rocks aren't soft.

But oh, my.
I'm so glad I did it!
On my second zip, I even opened my eyes.

The experience itself was really breathtaking. But even cooler than stepping outside my fear was saying in a cocky, it-doesn't-really-matter voice, *"Yeah. I went zip lining today. No big deal. … I was doing it with girlfriends."* Friends I had just met.

And let me tell you. Some intense bonding can take place rather quickly when some of us are wondering how big our bottom half looks in a contraption that fits tightly around our thighs while leaving our butts sticking out for all the world to notice!

We were girlfriends at a retreat, sharing moments, laughing, crying, talking about Jesus, and eating a whole lot of chocolate. Reflecting on real life. Telling our stories. Whispering from our hearts about our somethin's. (Because everybody's got somethin', right?)

And …
We were choosing to live outside our somethin'—our messy places—because **that's what God intends us to do.** We were reminding each other that life is bigger than our small world, and we don't need to stay in a rut, and it is OK to laugh and giggle and not think about those not-easy things for a while.

We lifted our faces to the sun, voices to the heavens, ankles to the tree tops, and our arms to each other and bathed in the warmth and love of friendship. And we zip lined.

This is Livin'!

Sometimes, it's easy to sit in the worries and responsibilities of today. We get too comfortable and settled with the chair and the space and the routine. *Then it gets harder to break the inertia.* But you know, girlfriends? We gotta' move! We can't spend all our time in the tough places, even when they are places that,

ironically, feel safe. There are some messy places that we can freely choose to leave.
Celebrate what is good and right in your world.

Let's. Have. Some. Fun.

Move out of your chair.
Dance with your girlfriends.
Zip line.

Please Give Me...

Her cheeks were flushed, and her neck was covered with the red blotches that I knew all too well. Her name tag read "Renee – Trainee," and I think the reindeer antlers she wore on her head made her feel even more self-conscious as she tried to figure out how to enter "no whip" on my hot chocolate order.

Oh, Jesus, please help her remember that this is just one day. Bring grace-filled people into her line this afternoon.

The lady in the purple parka with the big hood could have used a cart. Or a counter. Or a shelf. Anything on which she could rest the six or seven boxes she was trying to balance in her arms. But the line at the post office extended out the door to the sidewalk and we were at the back end of it. The purple parka lady was clearly ready for this day to be over. Her murmurs and her fussing and tear-filled eyes all signaled, "Enough already!"

Oh, Jesus, please give her the strength to just keep putting one foot in front of the other. Bring people into her path that will share her burdens—especially those in her heart.

The blonde, curly haired little boy, strapped in the shopping cart with a half-eaten ginger cookie crumbling in his hands could-not-stop-crying. Perhaps "wailing" is the better word. His mom was trying everything to calm him down, but he was beyond the calming down point. It was all too much for both of them. Another young mother spoke a few words of encouragement to the weary mama in the check-out line. But her hope of holding it together was weakening.

Oh, Jesus, please give that mama a special dose of patience today. Remind her that she is not defined by well-behaved or past-the-naptime children. Bless her with hugs and kisses when this moment passes.

'Tis the season ...
Lines seem to go on for days ...
Customer service employees can't keep up no matter how hard they try ...

Programs and parties and events require more energy than we really have …
Traffic snarls and crawls and keeps us from getting to where we want to be when we want to be there.

Oh, Jesus, please remind me that during these days, to-do lists will take longer. People are tired. We're trying to do too much too fast.

Show me how to be Grace. Patience. Compassion.

Name … Name … Name

Oh, the name. If I could only (always) remember the person's name. But I usually don't.

Too often I'll meet someone and panic sets in. The face. I know her. How do I know her … name … name … name …

I start searching through the contact list that sits in the gray mass covered by my not-so-natural blonde hair. Which category? Church? Speaking event? Client? Friend? Sister? (Ha! Just kidding.)
Name … name … name …

My most embarrassing *"I can't believe I didn't remember your name"* moment unfolded like this …
I walked into Caribou Coffee and saw a familiar face sitting at one of the tables. Mentally, I tried to connect the face with a name. I walked up to him and his friends and said, "Hi, John! Nice to see you again!" With a puzzled look on his face, he replied, "My name is Dave. I live across the street from you."

Good grief.

We've discussed the weather in the middle of the street between our houses. We've been in his home.

I mean, really. Good grief.
How could I forget his name?

And then I read about this Amazing God who doesn't know what it's like to forget someone's name. And because this whole remember-the-name-thing is such a challenge for me, I am really, really impressed and humbled by Isaiah 43:1, *"But now, this is what the Lord says, 'I have called you by name.'"*

This is The God who knows a bazillion people, right? And **He calls me by my name**.

This loving God whose heart beats for me and for you, He knows me. He knows you. And He loves us.

Who am I to doubt God's love for me? Why would I ever think that God doesn't know what's going on in my simple little life? How could I begin to believe that He has forgotten about me?

He calls me by my name.

This is really cool.

Only in the Movies

Really. On what planet does this happen?

A beautiful young woman wraps her thin sweater tightly around her shivering shoulders and staggers through the downpour. Her head leans into the swirling wind as she tries to get her bearings. The raindrops are sharp and icy cold. With no hood for protection, her face and hair are getting a beating. As she stumbles through the rushing torrent, she contemplates life with or without the man she is madly in love with. Should she marry him? Should she say *"no"*?

The camera circles her in a frenzy as we watch the tension in her face and feel her swirl of emotions.

Then, she makes up her mind. He-is-the-one. Ignoring the rainstorm and the puddles, she rushes to his apartment, into his arms, and she looks … well, she looks like she just stepped out of the hair and make-up chair.

Gorgeous, wet (perfect!) curls frame her rosy cheeks. Thick mascara has stayed on her eyelashes. Eyeliner still makes her eyes "pop." Her lips are glossy and tinted. Stunning.

Good grief.
In my world …

When I come out of the rain, I look like a drowned rat. My hair lays limp against my head. There's no color in my cheeks; I'm a very unattractive shade of ashen. My lips are blue; it's usually cold in the rain, you know. The mascara has found its way down my cheeks. (So much for paying extra for waterproof.) And rushing into the house? I'd probably fall on my butt. (Shoes get a little slippery after walking through water puddles, right?)

Only in the movies.

I'm surprised that a Hallmark TV scene that took maybe two minutes to watch has gotten a little rise out of me. I think it's because I'm tired of seeing actors portray the "not real" and try and pass it off as "real."

It becomes so easy to buy into the false advertising, doesn't it? Ridiculous expectations. The result? We spend too much money trying to find the right products and styles that keep us looking just like the unreality of the movies.

I will never, ever look like someone who just stepped out of "hair and make-up" when I've walked in the rain. But my short, limp hair will be easy to dry. My less-is-more make-up will be easy to wipe off. And I will love sloshing into my home where there's love, dry clothes, and warm socks.

Let's enjoy each day just as we are, without "hair and make-up" expectations.

Real life.
Cuz *This is livin'!*

When Life Becomes the List

"Domestic Goddess" will never be my title.
Becoming Suzy Homemaker is a dream. (More often, my experience is a nightmare.)
Every time I cook I pray that nobody dies from the food I've just prepared.

So a list of to-do's (The List) that involves cleaning, shopping, and cooking snatches me away from my happy place. It's a list of things I don't consider fun.

Sometimes, I put pretty blue bullets next to each group of words on The List to make it a bit more energizing. (Yeah, like that really works.) Sometimes, I scrawl The List on the back of a bank statement envelope (which just adds another whole layer of anxiety) with a broken pencil I find underneath the car seat, along with 13 pennies and two Life Saver candies. Sometimes, I start The List with everything I did yesterday just so I have a few tasks to cross off. (Some call it cheating. I call it creative list building.)

The List draws every ounce of air out of my lungs. It has more suction than that vacuum cleaner that can lift a bowling ball off the floor.

Furniture to dust. Floors to wash. Toilets to scrub. Rugs to be shaken. Cobwebs to be eliminated. Groceries to be bought. Carpets to be cleaned. Laundry to be moved from the washer to the dryer before it gets moldy. Or moldier.

Lord, in all of this busy-ness, please show me ...
How to live fully when life is reduced to The List.

And maybe most importantly ...
Tell me it's OK to just stop and breathe.

I put so much pressure on myself. Be. Do. Get It Done.
And these homemaking tasks don't come easily for me.

Please help me find that place of domestic contentment where I'm refreshed and not ragged.
Focused and not frazzled.
Settled and not sinking.

Lord, I know you meet me right where I am.

So, today, I'll see You at The List.

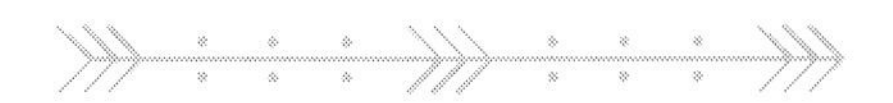

School Carnival. Climax, Minnesota. 1973.

The school carnival was an annual event where the high school classes each selected a guy and a gal as class representatives. The students sold tickets, and the representatives from the class who sold the most tickets were crowned king and queen. Teachers got soaked in the dunk tank, cheap stuffed animals and plastic gizmos were won in the gym, and the cake walk was celebrated in the cafeteria. Much fun was had by all.

I wore a purple hot pants outfit that year. With a purple headband. And purple tights. The outfit was … purple.

Good grief. Whatever was I thinking.

Back then, I felt like royalty. The look made me feel beautiful, even a little trim. Now it's one of those memories that makes me smile.

There are some memories, like purple hot pants, that just cause us to shake our heads and remember those times as typical growing up stories. Not a big deal. They are the stories we embellish and laugh about at school reunions. Permission is given to tease, make-fun-of, and joke about them with those who knew us back then.

But there are also the memories of words or events that bring a stinging pain to our hearts. These are not remembered fondly. "We don't talk about that" at the reunions.

It was in those tougher times that life got messy. And nothing can ever change those stories. The memories are just that … memories.

So what do we do with those memories and that pain? How do we move to a place where the pain isn't so cutting and the emotion isn't so raw even after 5, 10, 25, or 50 years? How do we keep the messy memories from binding our hearts and ruling our emotions today?

We choose to forgive.

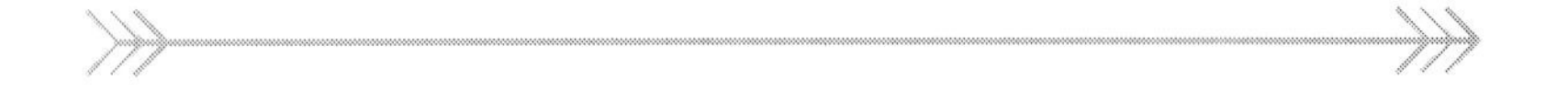

Oh, such a tough thing to do sometimes. Because these aren't the purple hot pants memories we're struggling with.

Here's what I lean on when memories from long ago (or yesterday) bump me from my happy place and move me to a place of hurt, guilt, anger, and bitterness—**God forgives me.**

Oh, the beauty of this. To be loved by a God who looks beyond my failures and my hurtful actions. It's such a gift.

> *"For as high as the heavens are above the earth, so great is his love for those who fear him; as far as the east is from the west, so far has he removed our transgressions from us." (Psalm 103:11-12)*

Take His promise as truth. The One who knows every single awful detail of that event will forgive every single awful consequence of that event. The words. The actions. All of it … FORGIVEN.

And when we accept God's forgiveness, the memory will lose its power over us.

Theologian and writer Frederick Buechner observes …

> *"The sad things that happened long ago will always remain part of who we are just as the glad and gracious things will too, but instead of being a burden of guilt, recrimination, and regret that make us constantly stumble as we go, even the saddest things can become, once we have made peace with them, a source of wisdom and strength for the journey that still lies ahead. It is through memory that we are able to reclaim much of our lives that we have long since written off by finding that in everything that has happened to us over the years God was offering us possibilities of new life and healing which, though we may have missed them at the time, we can still choose and be brought to life by and healed by all these years later."*

Reliving the tragedy, walking through the if-only's, carrying the blame and the shame—that will never, ever change what happened. We cannot rewrite history.

But we can learn to make different and better choices today because of our past experiences. We can create a better life if we choose to forgive ourselves.

And then, we forgive others.
Forgiving others who have hurt me is tough. I wish God didn't require this. It seems too big. Too unfair. Justice seems to be lost and "the other person gets away with it" if I release the pain and forgive. And yet, God is clear. Forgiveness is part of His desire

in wanting us to live in relationship first with Himself, and then with each other. Forgiveness is not about letting the other person off the hook, it's about getting my heart right with God.

> *"Bear with each other and forgive whatever grievances you may have against one another. Forgive as the Lord forgave you." (Colossians 3:13)*

Forgiveness isn't forgetting. Forgiveness is ending the blame. And ending the blame enables us to move forward without holding that moment—its hurts, bitterness, and judgement—as the moment that frames today.

Our lives are made up of moments, aren't they? Moments filled with joy, creating memories that make us smile. And moments filled with conflict, creating memories that make us sad.

We have a choice.
Live in the past with its hurt—bringing that hurt into today's moments and relationships—
Or …
Forgive ourselves and each other for the past—bringing that grace and forgiveness into today's moments and relationships.

My purple hot pants make for a fond memory. Other not-so-fond events or memories from years ago? I haven't forgotten them, and some still make me sad. But they aren't stumbling around in my story today.

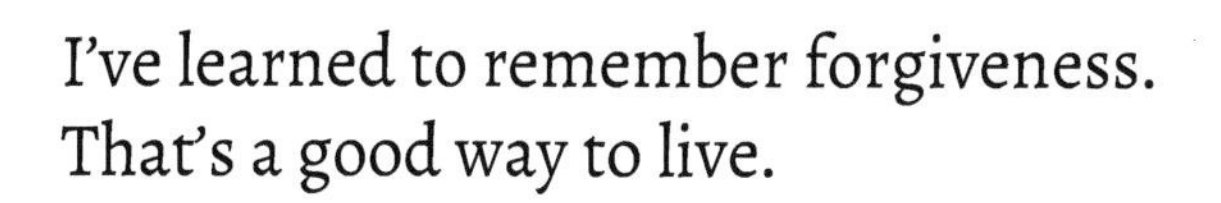

I've learned to remember forgiveness.
That's a good way to live.

"Hip replacement that includes a hiking schedule."

The billboard words convinced me that if I ever need a new hip (which I don't), that is the medical facility where I'd want to have the surgery. Why? The advertisers give me hope. They don't just tell me the surgery will go well. They help me anticipate the good things that will happen after the surgery.

The medical facility's advertisement paints a picture of how much better my life could be if I turn my pain and suffering over to their doctors.

My immediate "sign-me-up-now" reaction based on a billboard challenged my "do-your-research-first" decision making process. I don't know anything about the kind of work that particular hospital does. Haven't talked to anybody who has had a hip replaced there. Don't know anything about their success rate.

And yet, I feel I can trust them, and if necessary, could pick up the phone and call them for an appointment if I needed a new hip.

Why don't I have that same level of trust in my faith journey?

My God Who Loves Me Most—the One who would rather die

for me than live without me, the God who has answered my prayers, shown me miracles, and painted a thousand pictures for me in His Book about how He wants to bless my life with Peace, Hope, and Joy, the One whose billboard says, *"I have come to give you life abundantly…"* (John 10:10), He gets my worry prayers.

You know, those "worry prayers," the pleadings that tell Him I'm nervous about leaving my pain and hurts and worries with Him, believing that I need to do something to help Him out. Those prayer intentions that I leave at His feet and then, turn around and keep worrying about. Ooftah.

In a letter to other Christians who *"believe all the right things and still live the wrong way,"* James tells them/us to *"Ask boldly, believingly, without a second thought. People who 'worry their prayers' are like wind-whipped waves." (James 1:6 THE MESSAGE)*

I'm one of those people (oh, ye of little faith) who worries my prayers. I'm a wind-whipped wave.

If I had a hip problem, I'd be ready to put my pain in the hands of a particular medical facility because of seven words I saw on a billboard while driving down Interstate 694. But I leave, take back, worry…leave, take back, worry…leave, take back, worry…when bringing my real pains and hurts to The One True God.

Good grief.

I am so glad that God allows me to keep coming back. He never becomes impatient with me. **He's always there, waiting to hear all prayers, even my worry prayers.**

Thank you, God, for being a really Big God. Thank you for promising much, much, much bigger things than a hiking schedule after hip surgery.

I had come to the conclusion that the gentleman in seat 6F behind me was never going to stop talking.

His one-way conversation with the young man buckled in next to him (and everyone else within the vicinity of Row 6), covered an interesting blend of topics: the weather, the conference he was going to attend, his frustrations with his current work assignment, his political perspectives, and a whole lot more.

It felt as if his voice was perched on the top of my head—no breaths … an intense, sharp tone … and a steady stream of words tapping my brain like a woodpecker. RELENTLESS. And we were only at the point in our flight where the flight attendant was reminding us that our seat cushions could be used as flotation devices. (Since we were flying from Kansas City to Dallas, I'm not sure which large body of water we'd be diving into.)

And then … a few moments of sweet respite as his coffee was delivered. (Yes!)

His unyielding wordiness reminded me of how much of my day is spent taking in … stuff. Some of the stuff is good—information. Healthy conversations. Reminders. Heart encouragements. Learnings.

And then there's the blah blah blah stuff—irrelevant noise. Mindless TV. Phone conversations and emails and social media reads that I get lost in. Sensationalistic news. Stuff that keeps me from what matters most.

Later in the flight, as the flight attendant picked up our empty pretzel packages and plastic cups of melted ice cubes, I read this passage on my Kindle, written by contemplative writer Ed Cyzewski:

> *"... **every addition to our life requires a subtraction.** If you're trying to add something to your life without subtracting something else, there's a good chance the stuff that's already there will win... Sometimes we have very good things in our lives that have taken up an unhealthy amount of space. However you want to classify these things, we need to subtract the things that make it difficult to add prayer and writing to our lives."*

Hmmm ... I considered what I could add and what I could subtract. What changes could I make in my life that would bring more nourishment to my soul? More life-enriching activities. Less blah. Like reading more stimulating books instead of Facebook news highlights. Taking a wake-me-up walk outside instead of watching mindless TV.

Well, "Woodpecker" continued his one-way conversation in the clouds for 90 minutes. I took care of the brain tapping with a couple of Advil®. And we didn't need to use our seat cushions for anything other than providing comfort to our bottoms.

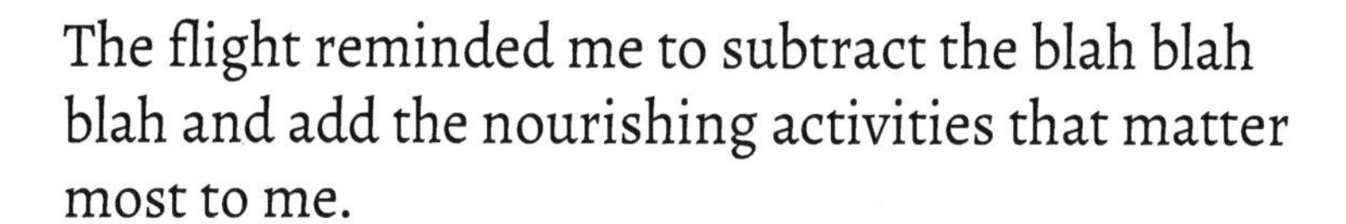

The flight reminded me to subtract the blah blah blah and add the nourishing activities that matter most to me.

Yup. I can do this.
Subtract. Then add.

"Hope! How blessed sounds that word."

That's one of my favorite lines from the melodrama *Love Rides the Rails* by Morland Cary. The story follows the scheming and deceptive tricks of villainous Simon Darkway. He wants to control the Walker Valley, Pine Bush & Pacific Railroad. And to do that? He tries to take advantage of its owner, Widow Hopewell, and her beautiful daughter, Prudence, the heroine. The good guy in the story? Truman Pendennis. (At the end of the story, Truman is tied to the tracks and Prudence saves him. Love that part.)

Anyway….
Prudence despairs when she learns of Simon's treachery, and in her despair she begins to faint. She whispers, "Hope! How blessed sounds that word," as she holds her thin wrist against her pale forehead and very gracefully glides to the ground.

Been there. Done that. Perhaps not quite as dramatically and with such lady-like flair as Prudence, but I'm no stranger to feelings of despair, and those words sure have been whispered from my lips. You, too?

We hope for a lot of things in life. We hope we finish the big project in time. We hope that people show up to our event. We hope the Minnesota Vikings win the Super Bowl. We hope…we wish. There's not too much despair involved. (Well, maybe the Vikings winning the Super Bowl involves some desperation.)

It's in my faith journey where real despair can start to settle in. The news is bad. Relationships are strained. The work never ends. And God is silent.

That's when Hope becomes more than a wish. It is not a dream. It is stronger than a whisper and a precursor to fainting. Hope becomes a lifeline. An anchor.

> *"Show me your ways, O Lord, teach me your paths; guide me in your truth and teach me, for* ***you are God, my Savior, and my hope is in you all day long."***
> *(Psalm 25:4-5)*

Our hope is based on a Supreme Someone who is rock solid. Someone who will not let us down.

And here's the thing…
Even when my prayer is not answered in the way I desire, my hope is still in Him. I still trust Him. That's what makes my hope in Him different than a wish for something. I do not despair, because HE is still my all-knowing, all-loving God. He has not forsaken me. He knows my heart, my disappointment, and the bigger picture. God, my Savior, does not fail me.

We serve a big God who loves us and wants us to confidently wait for Him to meet us with what we need in the moment.

"Let us hold unswervingly to the hope we profess, for he who promised is faithful." (Hebrews 10:23)

There are lots of villains out there, threatening to take away our peace, joy, and what matters most to us.

So let us hold unswervingly to hope.
He who promised is faithful.

It was part of the Sunday ritual growing up. Almost sacred—
The Afternoon Naps.

After church we'd eat the roast, mashed potatoes, corn, and rolls at the dining room table in the living room, using the glass water goblets and fancy plates. Then we would take a nap ... in our slips.

This remains a mystery. Why did we nap *in our slips*? They certainly weren't comfortable. Or warm. Or cozy. But we did.

Afternoon naps are still a big part of my Sunday. (Steve calls them my "third quarter snooze," in honor of my love for the game of football.)

I feel badly for those who can't nap. Because tight shoulders, heavy hearts, strained muscles, weariness—these all seem to loosen up with a nap.

I think that when Jesus says, *"Come, and I will give you rest,"* He is including naps.

I believe Jesus meets me in my slumber, in my resting, in my stopping my busy-ness.

I am praying for you, girlfriend. That you will find the rest you need.
Maybe you can find it in a nap?

The storm in your heart. When it reaches that fevered, frenzied pitch, and you believe you can't take one more minute of its torment ... *Lord, have mercy.*

It's similar to a storm in a Minnesota summer. Lightning strikes like physical pain—jolts of electricity that are jarring, piercing, immobilizing. Booming thunder from the sky shakes your foundation. Deafening, threatening noise drowns out all other reasonable voices. Rain whips horizontal and hurts. Sharp bits of water slash the earth and puncture all protection. Wind pummels from every side, destroying your sense of balance and ability to stand upright.

It's a storm. And a tough one.

In Minnesota, we have to ride out the summer storms.

But the storm in our hearts? Not so easy to ride THEM out.

We've lost power. So much darkness. We've lost energy. Nothing to plug into. Uprooted trees and debris keep us from moving forward. We're stuck. Stranded. Scared. And the wind and the rain keep beating...pummeling...defeating.

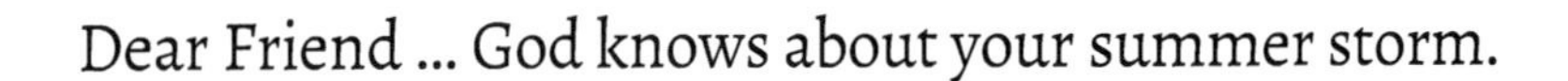

Dear Friend ... God knows about your summer storm.

He sees you huddled in the cellar, hoping the roof doesn't collapse.

He sees you standing in the slashing wind and rain, clenched fists and defiant heart, cursing the darkness, the noise, the pain.

He sees you scrambling in the blackness, tripping over life's routine as you search for a flashlight to pierce the darkness.

And wrap your heart around this ...
God is not standing outside the storm, hoping.
He has not dashed to a safe place for a change of dry clothes.

God is standing in the storm with you.
Bailing water. Carrying the flashlight.
Wrapping you in the rain slicker.

Calming the storm.
The summer storm in your heart.

Psalm 18 …

"In my distress I called to the Lord…
He reached down from on high and took hold of me;
He drew me out of deep waters…
He rescued me because He delighted in me."

God is faithful …
Always.

It was ***that*** sound.

You know, the one that wakes you up and revs your adrenaline big-time? You find yourself standing next to your bed in the dark wondering what strange thing is going on in the house, deciding if you should run or grab the lamp to defend yourself.

I stood perfectly still, wide-awake, heart racing, and listened carefully. I heard it again.

And then, I recognized it. It was my mom singing. Good grief.

Here's the back story …

A few months ago, mom concluded that talking was just taking too much energy. So she decided she didn't want to talk anymore. My sisters and I still aren't sure if she really was just too tired to talk, or if she was just being stubborn. Perhaps both. It was clear she was capable of talking because she would tell us. *"Of course, I can talk,"* she would say with indignation. But during this particular period of her life, she preferred to point to what she needed and whisper her requests.

Let me just say, as much as we love and care for our mom and her short-term memory and cognitive challenges, we found this to be so *annoying*.

My sister, Lori, stayed with mom one weekend. We say that *Lori hums her way through life*. Her heart spills out with joy, and in the daily routine, it shows up in her humming and singing around the house. Well, as Lori hummed, mom started humming along with her. Smart Lori decided to work with that and asked mom to sing some of the old hymns with her. Talk had returned!

Mom refers to this short period of time as "the time I couldn't talk." And since then, she has determined to practice talking. She considers singing her practice time.

Often in the morning after breakfast, we will sing a couple of hymns with her. Early on in these practice moments, I suggested we sing *How Great Thou Art* with Sandy Patti. Not a good idea. Mom attempting to sing in that 13 octave range that Spectacular Sandy has was a bit much. So then I tried her favorite hymn, *In the Garden,* singing along with Helen Reddy, in a much lower voice. Much better.

She also practices in her bed at night, singing the old southern Gospel songs with the Hallelujah TV music channel. I love hearing her sing along with those great songs, knowing that it's strengthening her muscles, helping her memory, and bringing good, refreshing messages into her heart … and ours. (I say our hearts because the TV volume is usually blaring, and it's as if I'm sitting right in front of The Bill Gaither Vocal Band sound system without ear plugs!)

Back to my night terror …
Mom wakes up a lot during the night because her memory challenges mess with her sleep patterns and internal clock. On

this particular night, she decided to practice singing when she woke up at 2:37 a.m. Loudly. In a very high vocal range. My mind didn't recognize it as singing. It registered more like a crying or a howling.

"Just a closer walk with Thee…"

From the belly.
Good grief.

The events of that evening remind me of two Bible verses:

"I will sing of the Lord's great love forever; with my mouth I will make your faithfulness known through all generations." (Psalm 89:1)

"I will lie down and sleep in peace..." (Psalm 4:8)

Mom's got both of these down, perfectly.
Me?
I'm still working on sleeping in peace.

Life Over Chips and Salsa

Some of life's most important conversations take place over chips and salsa.

(My first conversation with my now-husband Steve was on a blind date at Chi-Chi's Mexican restaurant so this statement has been scientifically proven to be true.)

Most recently, La Casita Restaurant provided the aqua-and-coral colored wall tiles, hanging sombreros, and mariachi music that framed another of life's moments.

My friend, Stephanie, and I were catching up about our families, our faith journeys, and our businesses over a beef burrito, fish tacos, and chips and salsa. (Keep them coming, thank you very much.) Talking about the things that mattered most to us.

I was struggling with business questions that were connected to my insecurities, life's busy-ness, and distractions that were taking me away from knowing God's heart on the issues. *What am I supposed to do? How do I do it? What if I can't do it?*

Stephanie's advice was perfect:

"Set aside all the details and questions that have you spinning. Get yourself grounded again. Make your relationship with The One Who Knows Best your highest priority."

How many times have I read Matthew's words that say the same thing. *"Seek first the kingdom of God and his righteousness, and all these things will be given to you as well." (Matthew 6:33)*

Yes.

(Let's take a short off-road trip down Memory Lane for just a moment. That verse from Matthew takes me back to Bible camp days. Does anyone else hear the pretty Alleluia descant music in your head when you read "Seek ye first the kingdom of God and His righteousness?" Love that descant!)

Anyway.
Stephanie's advice begins the best to-do list ever. Seek Him first.

This is one of the Bible verses we talked about around the campfire when tender hearts were saying *"Yes"* and God never felt more real, and in high school when we were really thinking about what it meant to follow Jesus and wondering if "all these things" included finding a boyfriend.

This is the verse to help figure out life's next steps when girlfriends encourage one another as they contemplate *what could be* over chips and salsa.

I'm learning to heed those words. Live them out. Read them and apply them.

Breathing is easier now. Waiting for answers isn't as difficult.

Seek Him ... and the rest will fall into place.

"If God gives such attention to the appearance of wildflowers—most of which are never even seen—don't you think he'll attend to you, take pride in you, do his best for you? What I'm trying to do here is to get you to relax, to not be so preoccupied with getting, so you can respond to God's giving. People who don't know God and the way he works fuss over these things, but you know both God and how he works. Steep your life in God-reality, God-initiative, God-provisions. Don't worry about missing out. You'll find all your everyday human concerns will be met.

Give your entire attention to what God is doing right now, and don't get worked up about what may or may not happen tomorrow. God will help you deal with whatever hard things come up when the time comes." (Matthew 6:30-34, THE MESSAGE)

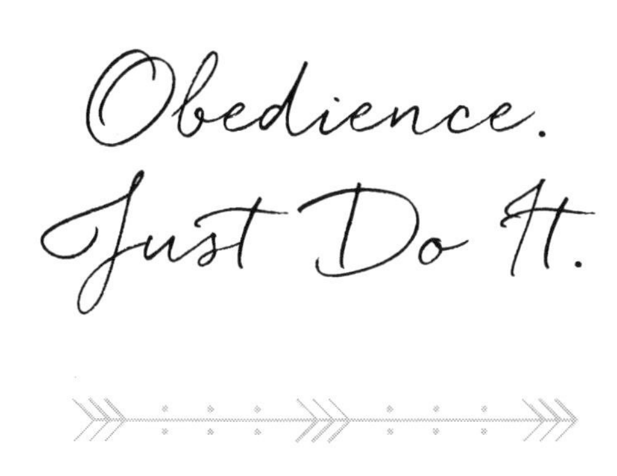

The lady with the infectious smile standing next to me giggled and said, *"Your feet are flat on the ground, Gaye. You don't have anything to worry about."*

We were watching a few of our fellow campers at the women's retreat navigate their steps across the high cable from the security of safe, firm ground. Well actually, I was watching only part of the time. Sometimes, I had to stop and turn away because looking up at them swaying in the wind made me a bit nervous. To say I was impressed with their courage and strength is putting it mildly.

These braver-than-I-was girlfriends climbed the utility pole, then shimmied sideways across a narrow cable while keeping their balance by holding onto another cable that found a rhythm of its own about 20 feet above the earth. When their daring walk was done and they had reached the other side of the cable, they needed to get back to the ground. And how did they do that? They sat on a 1'x3' platform, folded their arms across their chests, and then rolled off.

Yeah. Rolled off. A cable that was hooked to their waist gently swung them to the ground.

Good grief.

The guy in charge of this retreat exercise made it clear to these cable gliders—once you sit on that itty bitty platform and cross your arms, ***roll off right away.*** If you think about it too much, it will be very difficult to actually complete the roll.

The symbolism in that instruction wasn't lost on me.

The scenario describes part of my faith journey.
Obedience.

When God gives me clear direction and it involves doing something scary, or if I don't feel qualified, my natural tendency is to think about it. In great detail. For a long time. And thinking about it keeps me from actually following the direction. It keeps me from rolling off the platform into Trust. And the more I think about what He's calling me to do, and I begin to procrastinate about it, the more I actually convince myself that I'm not ready. Not good enough. Not strong enough.

And then in my presumption, I question God's direction. (I should really know better.)

And then my indecision can turn into disobedience.

Sigh.

The ladies who braved the high wire showed me what faith and obedience look like. How the two work together. These gals had faith in their guide, trusted the plan, and responded immediately to what they were told to do.

Their reward?
They had an AMAZING adventure.

Faith and obedience.
Cable walking and God trusting.
This is livin'!

You will never hear these comments leave the lips of Olympic skiers:

> *"Do these ski pants make my butt look big?"*
> *"Who's bringing donuts to warm-ups tomorrow?"*
> *"Gonna' have me a big ol' bowl of Haagen-Dazs tonight to celebrate the prelims!"*

Can you even imagine those thoughts being seriously considered by an Olympian? No. These athletes are committed and focused. Their discipline is over-the-top impressive. That is why they can fly down the slopes with a death-defying command of their skis, and an excitement and confidence that replaces any fear.

Speed. Skill. Fearlessness.
Wow.

My first downhill skiing experience was not anything like that.

Snowplow with me back to those thrilling days of yester-year… After riding the chairlift to the top of the not-very-steep hill, I panicked. I didn't get off the lift when I was supposed to, and I began riding it back down the hill. Panicking again, I realized this was pretty stupid, so I jumped off the lift. Landed on the roof of a small hut.

Trying to get off the hut's roof in skis? Not-attractive-at-all. (Yeah, I know. Why not take the skis off?)

My second attempt at conquering the downhill was 10 plus years later. Again, good grief.

This experience was a ski trip with a group of friends. I was more worried about looking too bulky in my ski attire than I was about getting back on skis. I should have worried about the skiing.

After taking, oh, about 45 minutes to get down the not-very-steep hill, one of my friends took pity on me. I spent the rest of the afternoon skiing behind him. I mean **right behind him.** My skis glided between his, my hands were on his waist, and my face was between his shoulder blades.

So. Not. Cool. And not very fun. I could probably describe every colorful stitch on the back of his smartly designed ski jacket. But I could not tell you anything about the snow, trees, or skiers on the hill.

There is a distinct difference between the experiences of those gutsy, passionate US skiers and my bunny hill slides. Besides the obvious contrast in athleticism. They are working hard, and **they're having fun.** This is an experience they will remember for a lifetime, and ***they're living every moment out loud.***

I am working hard and staying in a place of fear and panic, hoping the moment will end soon or that Jesus will come quickly.

I want to live moments like the Olympians.

Obviously, my moments won't be on the slopes. But in my work, in my relationships, and in my playtime, I want to approach and live my moments with passion and energy.

Caribou Coffee reminds us that *Life is Short. Stay awake for it.* ™

Yeah. That's what I want. At the end of the day, I want to stand on my little step-up exercise box, raise my arms above my head, and say, *"Yes! Today I showed up and gave my moments everything I had. This is livin'!"*

Paul, a great leader of our church and encourager of our faith, wrote,

"I have fought the good fight, I have finished the race, I have kept the faith." (II Timothy 4:7)

Yeah.
That's what I want.

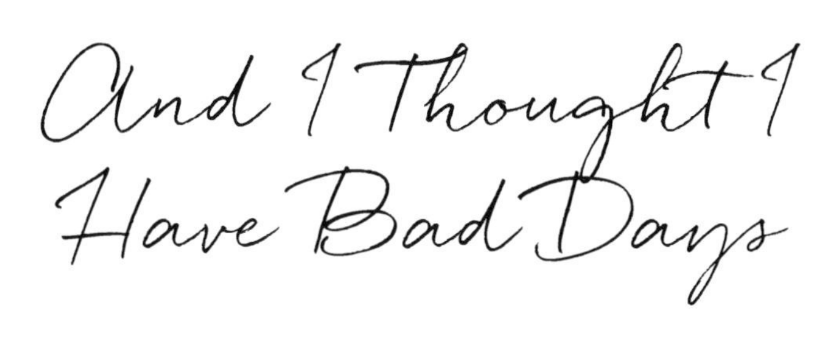

Have you read the book of Job in the Bible?
Amazing.

I whine and complain about a frustration with a client. A disappointing comment from a friend. A schedule that is interrupted by the unexpected—usually by people.

And then I read about Job.

> *"This man was blameless and upright; he feared God and shunned evil … He was the greatest man among all the people of the East." (Job 1:8)*

But here is what he dealt with …
His oxen and donkeys were attacked and killed by some horrible people.
His sheep were destroyed by a fire that fell from the sky.
His camels were carried off by a group of hoodlums.
His servants were killed.

And then the ultimate act of horror …
His ten children were killed when the roof of the house they were in collapsed on them.

The Bible says, *"At this, Job got up and tore his robe and shaved his head. Then he fell to the ground in worship...In all this, Job did not sin by charging God with wrongdoing." (Job 1:20-22)*

WOW.

It is really hard to get my head around Job's response. His ten children died in one afternoon. His sorrow was gut-wrenching. Unimaginable. And he fell on his knees and worshipped God. Can't even imagine.

Much of the book of Job focuses on conversations he had with his friends as they tried to console and support him. They first responded to Job's great sorrow and tragedy with sympathy. But as time went on, they tried to figure it out. They wanted to understand "why" Job was suffering. The result? Job felt condemned instead of comforted.

It makes me wonder if I ever respond to my girlfriends' pain as these friends did. In my desire to make my friends feel better, do I too quickly go to "fixing it" and "explaining it," rather than just being present in the pain? Is my interest in wanting them to feel better really selfishly motivated—I want to feel better? And I can't feel better until they feel better?

I've learned and relearned that I am not always supposed to fix the pain. So how should I respond when my friends experience sadness and overwhelming challenges? What is the best way for me to support them?

Job tells us what helped him in his out-of-control messiness. He needed to see God. *"My ears had heard you but now my eyes have seen you." (Job 42:5)*

I can help my friends in the same way. I can help them *see* God.
I am not called to *be* God.

As much as I'd like to "make it better" for them, I need to listen for God's guidance to know how best to support them. Sometimes, God may use me to encourage them. Sometimes, to provide advice. Always, to love them. Always, to show grace.

Job's story keeps my bad days in perspective and my heart humbled. It teaches me how to be a friend.

Here's how Job's story ends …

> *"After Job had prayed for his friends, the Lord made him prosperous again and gave him twice as much as he had before [14,000 sheep, 6,000 camels, 1,000 yoke of oxen, 1,000 donkeys, 7 sons, 3 daughters]…The Lord blessed the latter part of Job's life more than the first…After this, Job lived a hundred and forty years; he saw his children and their children to the fourth generation. And so he died, old and full of years." (Job 42:10-17)*

And again…WOW.

He Has a Plan

Ooftah.
I mean, really. Big Time Ooftah.

It was a torn anterior cruciate ligament (ACL), torn medial collateral ligament (MCL), multiple tears in the meniscus, a femur impaction fracture, and a bruised tibia.

Yes, you could say that her knee was "really messed up." You could also say that when my niece Kelsey plays basketball, she gives it everything she's got.

Kelsey is the athlete who loves playing basketball, the rhythm-finder who loves to dance and choreograph, and the high school senior who relishes each fun moment with her school buds. And as she tentatively negotiated her way through the Minnesota ice and snow with a large brace around her leg and crutches keeping her steady, she wore a smile that just didn't end.

Imagine the pain … and aren't we grateful for morphine. Morphine is one of those drugs that while it dulls the sharpness of the "make it stop now" lightning bolts of pain that surge through your body, it also brings you to a mental happy place that can act like truth serum.

When Kelsey received some morphine relief in the emergency room, she went to her happy place and whispered,
"God has a plan."

Her instinctive response still impresses me. Humbles me.
I wish my responses to Ooftah moments were filled with such faith.

My knee isn't a mangled mess, but life has its share of pain.

You too?

Muscles strain and stretch from carrying worry loads we aren't designed to carry. Feelings bruise from misunderstandings and words that hurt. Relationships fracture because we need to be right, and it's not fair that the other person can say those horrible things and get away with it. And a full-body weariness makes getting out of bed a gold-star achievement.

Wouldn't it be soul-changing, if ...
when our life is all mangled and strangled and hanging together by ligaments that only The Great Physician can diagnose and heal ...
that we would whisper ...
God has a plan.

I'm learning that I can trust this truth.
Trust that He has a plan.

God doesn't need time to schedule MRIs or review X-rays or talk to specialists. He knows exactly what our hearts need the moment we crumble to the floor, hit the emotional wall, or enter that dark place. He meets us **right where we are** and brings us to the right place. Healing. Peace. Comfort.
A place better than the one we left.

His **love** holds my heart together.
His **grace** allows me to lift my head.
His **presence** fills me with peace.
His **promises** give me hope for a better day.

He lifts my crumpled body from the basketball court, infuses my heart, mind, emotions, and soul with his healing touch, and tells me…

I have a plan. Just for you.

Just wait and see.

You and Agent Frank and Me

I spent a Friday afternoon sitting at my kitchen table with Agent Frank from the Geek Squad®.

Could a Friday afternoon get any more exciting than this? I mean, really—computer meltdowns spiraling and client deadlines passing. Bring out the Advil®! (I know. Why the Advil when I'm trusting Jesus to keep my head from exploding? Because I think there are times when Jesus and Advil make the perfect combo.)

I decide while watching Agent Frank tap those keyboard keys and speak a language that is definitely not English or Norwegian, that if I'm ever banished to a remote island and can take two people with me (not family or close friends), I will take a computer geek and a dentist. (The dentist is a whole other topic. And yeah, maybe the computer geek would be one of the two even if family or friends were included.)

Computer problems upend my world because I know absolutely nothing about them, and technical stuff makes me break out in a rash around my eyes, downright scary to those who see me. When that little blue circle just keeps spinning around and around and around in the center of my computer screen, I think of things not listed in Philippians 4:8 *"...whatever is true*

... noble ... right ... pure ... lovely ... think on these things."
You know what I mean, right?

But back to Agent Frank ...

As I'm watching him calmly and methodically look through all the hidden crannies of this *I can't live without it* piece of electronics, I realize he loves his work. And he's very good at it.

I marvel at the reminder...
How each one of us can show up every day with skills and abilities and interests and passions that belong *uniquely* to us. And in our uniqueness, we each make a difference. Isn't it amazing?

No one else can be Agent Frank.
No one else can be you.
No one else can be me.

Agent Frank shows up every day to do great things. You show up every day to do great things. I show up every day to do great things, except when I have computer problems.

Together, you and Agent Frank and I are changing the world.

Thank you for showing up.

A Trip to Whining

This type of road trip happens haphazardly, without any planning.

You get in the car and drive mindlessly, with no intended destination. You set the cruise control and your mind shuts down and you just keep driving without considering what's happening around you.

With this trip, though, I *subconsciously* have a destination in mind. I'm going to "My Whining Place," a place from which no postcards are sent.

The trip started so innocently. The car had gas. There wasn't much traffic. I didn't need the windshield wipers. But soon there were unexpected detours, closed rest stops, and treacherous potholes. And that initiated a few grumbles, murmurings, and complaining.

And pretty soon I was just … whining.

My Whining Place is not a place I deliberately visit. Or at least, I'd like to believe I don't. But there is a bit of comfort and familiarity there, like warm flannel pajamas with booties on a chilly, drizzly night.

Whining involves blaming someone else for my worn out spark plugs and thread-bare tires, also known as my emotions. Whining lets me sulk; it doesn't ask me to change. Whining tells me it's my right to be hurt, upset, frustrated.

What a waste of energy and time. Right? Right.

And here's the deal. I'm the only one who can make me leave My Whining Place. No one else can turn my Mercury Milan around and change my direction except me. No one shares the driver's seat with me.

So ...
Because whining makes me miserable ...
And really makes those around me miserable ...
It's time to change my destination.

Changing my thoughts.
Changing my heart.
Changing my words.

The choice is mine.

Philippians 3:14 tells us to *"Do everything without complaining or arguing..."*

The directions and expectations couldn't be any clearer. Stop whining.

Roger that, Lord. Heading home to My Happy Place.

I'm standing in front of the kale and spinach in the big box grocery store, apologizing over the phone for what seems to be the zillionth time in five days. It has been a week filled with messy moments.

A few minutes earlier, when I was placing a quart of two percent milk in my shopping cart, my sister called. She was trying to help me out with my schedule. But I was sharp and short. (And I'm not describing my appearance.)

I called her back when I got to the land of green veggies and explained I hadn't slept much the night before and I was tired. And then I changed the word tired to weary. And I said I was sorry.

And as she always does, Julie said, *"Don't worry about it … it's OK."*
I said, *"No, it's not. It's really not."*

Being weary may be a reason for my impatience and selfishness, but it's not an excuse. (Even the fact that shopping is #236 on my list of favorite things to do doesn't make it a good reason to snap.)

We all have our moments, don't we? In each of my "moments" I initially squirm and try to justify and rationalize my behavior in my head so that I don't have to apologize, because saying *"I'm sorry"* isn't easy.

But the squirming doesn't bring peace. And it keeps me from my happy place. It's just so much better to say "I'm sorry," and move away from the messy.

Life is too fleeting to live short and snappy.
And if I add feeling guilty and uncomfortable because of my words ... then life just gets miserable.

I am grateful for the grace that friends and family demonstrate with the words, *"That's OK."* For accepting the apology. For looking at my heart.

May I remember to extend that same grace in return.

Life is much better when *"I'm sorry"* is part of our conversation.

Who Made Up the Rule?

I wonder who made up "The Rule."
The Rule that dictates where women are supposed to stand when they wait in line in a public bathroom.

During break time at the conference we all dash to the restroom, right? But the dash comes to an abrupt halt when we open the door. There we find women crammed into a corner behind the door, elbow-to-elbow, because no one wants to actually move into the bathroom and stand in the open space between the row of stalls and the row of sinks.

I don't understand this.

There is plenty of room if we line up on the peach-colored tile in front of the sinks and the mirrors. Ladies are still able to move gracefully from stall to sink to towel dispenser without getting crushed by the masses.

But I guess one day long ago, one woman decided that no one should stand in that space. Maybe someone got in her way when she was trying to put on her lipstick. Or she feared that annoying women would try to butt in and we wouldn't remember who was really next in line. As a result, we must now all huddle behind the door or line up in front of the drinking fountain and registration table outside this important room.

Until. Oh my.
This happened.

During a break at a well-attended conference, one woman decided she'd had enough of the door hitting her in the forehead as she waited for a vacant stall. She boldly stepped out from behind the door, moved in front of several very warm and crowded women, and placed herself in the center part of the bathroom where there was plenty of empty space.

Oh, yes, she really did it.

She didn't look at anyone, just silently stood there and breathed deeply. She was my hero. Her cape may have been invisible, but I knew it was there.

I moved out of the doorway, pushed through the masses, and bravely stood next to her. I was Robin to her Batman, or Amazing Girl to her Wonder Woman.

We were taking a stand against the greatest annoyance in the history of FOREVER. We were Big Girls. Going where no woman had dared to go before. Unafraid. Bold. Changing the world one bathroom line at a time.

We stood there alone while the bathroom went silent (except for the frequent flushes and very obnoxiously loud hand dryers). No one else joined us. Everybody tried not to stare.

It was a brave moment. It was livin' at its best.
I'm hoping it will start a movement.

We can do this, girlfriends.
Let's break The Rule.
Let's find the open spaces and move in, not waiting for permission.
Let's be brave.

Piano has always been my thing. Singing? Not so much.

I'm great at finding the harmony, but I'm definitely not solo material. Put me in the back with a group, and I'm just fine. So when I stepped up to pinch hit with a vocal solo a few years back, I surprised even myself.

I was traveling with a girls' choir from a Teen Challenge center in New York. As a staff member, I was responsible for driving one of the vans, getting the women in place for the performance, and standing in the back of the room making large gestures to remind them to smile. At this concert, one of the women had to pull out at the last minute. She had a key solo.

No one was willing to step up and take that solo ... except me.

Good grief. What was I thinking.

The choir sang with background accompaniment tapes, so there wasn't any extra help available from someone sitting at a piano who could play a little louder during the solo. I was the only one in the choir holding a music book in my hands and the only one who wasn't wearing the standard uniform. I clearly stood out. Standing in the center of the front row, I sang the first verse to the song *Cup of Cold Water.* I gave it everything I had, knowing with every note that this was not my finest moment.

At the end of the concert, the other staff member managing the sound system walked up to me, put her hands on my shoulders, looked me in the eyes, and said, *"That was very brave of you."*

(I could read between the lines.)

But you know? It was brave. And I did it. I wish I had a picture of that moment. I would slap it on Instagram and Facebook and make a name badge out of it: "My name is Brave."

That moment is a very vivid memory. And what makes me high-five myself with an "Atta-Girl!"? I volunteered to solo, knowing my performance wouldn't be perfect, knowing that I wasn't ready.

How many times do I say "No" to opportunities, simply because I don't think my participation will be perfect? Good enough. Or I don't have the right thing to wear. Or the task seems too hard. Or I might look stupid or silly.

If I wait until I think I'm ready, or have it perfected, I'll never do it. I'll put it off with excuses. My soft, cushy comfort zone will be the place from which I peek out and wonder, *"What if?"* and *"They look like they're having fun ... maybe I could do it too?"*

Writing a book. Teaching Sunday School. Volunteering to plan the party. Initiating the difficult conversation. Joining the exercise group. (Believe me...you don't have to wear the perfect outfit to sweat. And you certainly don't have to be in shape first!)

Here's the deal. If you take a chance and you mess up, so what? The world is not going to turn upside down because you were brave enough to try something new. Your mess-up moment will pass, and you can pat yourself on the back, knowing that you tried. That's just part of growing up.

Care to join me?

Let's show up.
Sing the solo when we're not a soloist.
Create interesting life moments outside of our comfort zones.
And then take the pictures!

Some refer to the solo as a moment of amazement that defies talent. I refer to it as the time when my sister Lori was so tired of practicing that her brain froze up.

The event was the annual piano recital.

Here's a little set-up to the remarkable performance ...

His glasses were always perched on his forehead, and his legs were always crossed. Mr. Anderson was an extremely gifted piano teacher who reminded us that music was more than notes and that any God-given talent was intended to be developed. He would bang out our weekly lessons with his two index fingers on an antiquated black typewriter using carbon paper between the pages. He called each of us "Ole." When we weren't prepared (he *always* knew when we weren't prepared!), he'd type an "Ooftah" on our weekly lesson plan. I'm not kidding. He'd type "Ooftah."

Spring piano recitals were held in the basement of Mr. Anderson's home in Crookston, Minnesota. As little girls, Julie and Lori and I would practice and practice and practice for the annual performance. Stressed-out nerves would hit a crescendo the night before the big event. A whole lot of deals were proposed to God if he would just help us memorize and remember the piece *this one time.*

And now, to the big night …

It was Lori's turn to show the rest of us how much she had prepared. She was ready. At least she was until she sat down on the piano bench.

Lori started playing. But her right hand found a tempo that was very different from the tempo her left hand found. One hand was playing two measures faster than the other; one playing allegro, the other adagio. One was forte, the other pianissimo. (We had never heard this song during her hours of practice.)

She stopped. Paused. Started over. Once again, her right hand skimmed the keys faster than her left. She stopped. Paused. Started over. *Aaaannd*...it was as if her hands were each attached to two different people, each listening to a metronome set on a different speed.

The next and final time she started the song, she just kept playing. Two hands playing the same song in different tempos and different expressions. The confusion sounded nothing like music.

At the end of the song—well, when her left hand finally finished the song a few seconds after her right hand—she stopped playing, placed her hands in her lap, and just sat on the bench for a moment looking at the keys. The basement was completely still. Julie and I had stopped breathing. We clenched our little hands in our laps, wanting to just grab Lori and head for the cookies and punch.

Mr. Anderson took his glasses off his forehead, rubbed his eyes with his hands, and graciously murmured, *"Amazing. I've never seen anything like that."*

The minute Lori got home that evening, she sat down on the piano bench and played her song **perfectly.**

Life has felt like a botched recital for me at times. Everything just seems out of synch. No matter how many times I pause and start over, my rhythm is off. My lesson is filled with Ooftah's as I try and try and try again to find my equilibrium. But all the energy and effort I muster can't get me back on track. I just cannot get it together.

We've all had those moments, haven't we? We will have more of them, you know. Count on it.

The good news is; those messy moments will eventually end.

I've learned that the best action I can take in that messiness is to simply stop. My mind needs to reset. I need to take a deep breath. Walk away for a minute. Stop trying so hard. Maybe have some fruit and a veggie drink…or cookies and punch ...

And then begin playing again the next day. In synch.

This is livin'.
Learning to move from messy moments to happy places.

Purple Hot Pants Memories

Frederick Buechner, *Listening to Your Life: Daily Meditations with Frederick Buechner,* (HarperCollins Publishers 1992), 323-324.

Worry Prayers

"...believe all the right things and still live the wrong way..." *Women of Faith Study Bible: New International Version,* Jean E. Syswerda, General Editor, ZondervanPublishingHouse: Grand Rapids, MI, 2001, p. 2010

Blah Blah Blah

Ed Cyzewski, *Pray, Write, Grow: Cultivating Prayer and Writing Together.* (Self-published, 2015), Kindle, 17.

Hope for Prudence and the Rest of Us

Morland Cary, *Love Rides the Rails; or Will the Mail Train Run Tonight?* (Dramatists Play Service, Inc., 1998).

Naps

Matthew 11:28

Minnesota Summer Storm

Psalm 18, verses 6, 16, and 17

Twisted Tights

Tom Gundermann, *Forgive Me*. Used with permission.

Something Personal

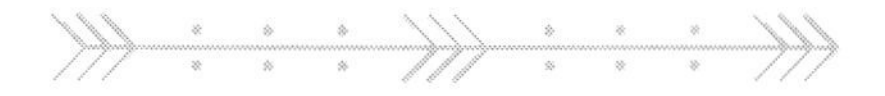

Because I love taking a peek into the personal world of the authors of the books I read, here's a glimpse into mine ...

I love to laugh and am not afraid to poke fun at my own mishaps. From my front row seat in life's theater, I've seen daily living meet uncommon grace—growing up in a small farming community, navigating through corporate corridors and board rooms, celebrating a whole bunch of good stuff, regaining my balance when the not-so-good stuff happens, and laughing and sharing tears with other women who want to live a faith-filled life in a world that demands so much. I shared some of these stories in my book, *God, Girlfriends & Chocolate.*

Before starting my own company in 2002, I spent 20+ years in human resources leadership positions in Fortune 500 companies, small businesses, and non-profit organizations. My experiences include leading a team that supported 11,000 airline employees, serving as Senior Vice President/Special Assistant to a College President, and leading organizational transitions in several companies.

I am privileged to serve as the Midwest Regional Director for Christian Women in Media, and to have served as president of the National Speakers Association – MN Chapter.

My favorite things? Music, books, chocolate, football, walks, naps, listening to jazz with my husband Steve, and laughing out loud 'til it hurts (especially with my sisters).

Steve and I live in St. Paul, Minnesota. My sisters and I take turns caring for and staying with my mom, as she learns to live with memory and cognitive challenges.

My faith journey matters to me. I love Jesus dearly, and am amazed at His unconditional love. His Grace, Mercy, Peace…WOW.

I've asked God to meet me a gazillion times in my joy and in my messiness. He's always shown up.

This is Livin'!

Dear Friend,

I wish we could share a veggie pizza or a hot fudge sundae. I'd smile into your eyes and whisper, "You are not alone. We can walk this journey called Life together." We'd share our stories, breathe deeply, and giggle a bit.

Until then…
If you're looking for encouragement and "Me too!" moments – more musings and observations on learning how to live a great life—you'll find me sharing mine at GayeLindfors.com. Maybe we could connect there as we move from messy moments to happy places. That would be nice.

Here are a few other places where I connect with friends like you…

Facebook: facebook.com/gayelindfors
Instagram: @gayelindfors
Pinterest: pinterest.com/gayelindfors
LinkedIn: gayelindfors
www.SignificantSolutionsInc.com

If you are looking for a speaker for your women's event, luncheon, or conference, let's talk. It would be a (fun!) privilege to partner with you.

With love and gratitude,
Gaye

Gaye@GayeLindfors.com
www.GayeLindfors.com